Everybody
Needs
Somebody
Sometime

*To Elise
with appreciation
of our continuing
friendship,
    warmly
      Jerry*

Everybody Needs Somebody Sometime

GERALD L. DAHL

THOMAS NELSON PUBLISHERS
NASHVILLE

Scripture quotations marked RSV are from the Revised Standard Version of the Bible, copyrighted 1946, 1952, © 1971, 1973.

Scripture quotations marked TLB are from *The Living Bible* (Wheaton, Illinois: Tyndale House Publishers, 1971) and are used by permission.

Scripture quotations marked NKJB–NT are from The New King James Bible–New Testament. Copyright © 1979 by Thomas Nelson Inc., Publishers.

Scripture quotations marked KJV are from the King James Version of the Bible.

Copyright © 1980 by Gerald L. Dahl

All rights reserved. No part of this book may be used or reproduced in any manner whatsoever without written permission of the publisher, except for brief quotations in critical reviews or articles. Printed in the United States of America.

Library of Congress Cataloging in Publication Data

Dahl, Gerald L
   Everybody needs somebody sometime.

   Includes bibliographical references.
   1. Christian life—1960– 2. Interpersonal relations. 3. Dahl, Gerald L. I. Title.
BV4501.2.D29   248.4   80–20247
ISBN 0–8407–5222–9

To Judy
With Love

Contents

ACKNOWLEDGMENTS
ix

1
A CASE FOR RELATIONSHIPS
11

2
IT'S YOUR CHOICE
15

3
POPULAR PEOPLE WITH NO FRIENDS
27

4
PHASE 1: ATTRACTION
39

5
PHASE 2: TESTING
54

6
PHASE 3: COMMITMENT
66

7
PHASE 4: MAINTENANCE
80

8
PHASE 5: ENDING
92

9
RESTORING RELATIONSHIPS
109

10
DON'T GO IT ALONE
126

11
GO IN PEACE
134

NOTES
144

Acknowledgments

These pages are filled with stories from the lives of real people. The names and situations have been changed to protect their confidentiality, but it all really happened. I want to thank these persons, as well as many others too numerous to list, for the truths they shared about relationships and how they work in our lives.

I am deeply appreciative of Alvera and Berkeley Mickelsen, who offered so much in God-given guidance for several important parts of this book. My personal gratitude goes to Barbara Katz for her valuable advice. Of equal importance was Carol Clarke's diligent help in typing the final manuscript. And then there is "Mimi," Mrs. Beryl Brown, my mother-in-law, who carefully reviewed the pages of this book and offered many helpful suggestions.

Now, as you begin to read, may you find that the events in the lives of the people of this book characterize your life as well. I pray that God will speak to you personally through these pages.

Gerald L. Dahl

Golden Valley, Minnesota
April 1980

1
A Case for Relationships

The day of the do-your-own-thing psychology is over, and the notion that you cannot form good relationships until you are well-adjusted personally is a myth. The truth is, your personal growth and happiness are the results of good relationships. If you are trying to solve your problems all alone at the expense of your relationships, there is a good chance you will stop growing as a person or experience even greater loneliness coupled with additional problems.

Some of your relationships may be destructive and should end. But routinely choosing to walk recklessly away from problem relationships places you on a hopeless merry-go-round. Even during your first days of life, as your pangs of hunger were sated, you learned an important lesson: Satisfaction comes from beyond one's self. You cannot find it alone.

As people undergo stress from their relationships, they are frequently advised, "That's not your problem, but theirs." Over and over in the clinical setting I have met people who do not accept their responsibility for the pain in a relationship, and therefore do not accept the fact that the stress is partially caused by internal factors they

EVERYBODY NEEDS SOMEBODY SOMETIME

can often change. Instead they abandon the relationship in an effort to find relief from the stress and tension it creates. In the end that tension is eliminated, but the relationship is finished as well. Only after a relationship has been abandoned does the sense of loss make one realize the true price that was paid.

Throughout the past twelve years, my experience in counseling has taught me that even as relationships are part of a person's problems, likewise they are also part of the solution. The answer is not to end relationships quickly when the going gets tough, but rather to recognize that they are worth the struggle to strengthen them. In so doing, the relationship will become the tool that restores a person's strength and well-being, even as it is in the process of growing itself.

I will always remember the young man who was one of my first patients. Intent upon demonstrating my competence, I carefully took all the right steps. After consultation with a colleague, I was convinced that I had a proper diagnosis and treatment plan. Session after session I applied counseling techniques fresh from my graduate school notebooks. Everything seemed on target, except for the fact that this person was not getting better.

Then to my amazement positive changes began to occur. The man's confidence began to return while symptoms of nervousness and anxiety were diminishing. I was puzzled, because I was not doing anything differently from before.

Curiosity forced me to set aside my professional facade and ask him outright, "What made the difference?" (I was hesitant to ask since I was under the illusion that any good therapist ought to know the answer.) I was expecting

A CASE FOR RELATIONSHIPS

him to point out certain counseling techniques or bits of insight from the past that had made the difference. But that wasn't it at all.

Instead he looked straight into my eyes and said, "I finally realized that you genuinely care about me and want me to get better." He knew I would stay with him until he was well, and in turn he was ready to work with me. We had a commitment to each other, a commitment to work together in therapy. In short, we had established a relationship.

The tools and techniques of counseling are important and useful; but the whole process does not have life until mutual commitment has been established. Committed relationships are a source of life and power to an individual. Oftentimes the person who comes into our clinic with emotional problems also has had a breakdown in his personal relationships. To start the process of growth, these relationships *must* be reestablished. In therapy, the counselee gains confidence as a result of the relationship with the therapist, and thus is enabled to revitalize or begin other relationships. It is the rebuilding of relationships, then, that fosters the personal strength in these people needed to maintain confidence and growth.

I often place couples with marital difficulties in a group therapy setting. They meet with four other couples each week and, predictably, positive changes occur. Why? Although counseling techniques both in group and private therapy are relatively the same, the crucial element—relationships with other caring couples—make all the difference. The mystique of the group is not methods or techniques, but people building relationships.

Don't be misled. Relationships are not important only

EVERYBODY NEEDS SOMEBODY SOMETIME

in the clinical scene. They are essential in *your* everyday life. The pace of modern life has made it all too easy to exist comfortably without others, to fill up the time and space they should occupy. Many people *know* they are lacking personal relationships, while others *think* they have good, vital ones when in reality they do not.

To complicate matters, we are living in a day of counterfeit relationships. These are nothing more than attractions without any form of commitment. Throughout life, we pass by one another but never truly connect. Restless, frustrated, and lonely, we are surrounded by people we know but do not know well. The patience and the desire to make the connection, to transform the counterfeit relationship into the real thing must be fostered in each one of us.

Today, throughout our crowded world, people such as yourself have more contact with one another than at any other time in history. Through travel, advanced communication, and daily business, people are continually interacting with each other. Yet, at the same time, these same people in record numbers are saying they have no one with whom to talk in times of crisis. Are you one of them? If so, I firmly believe that what will be said in the following pages will be of concrete help and encouragement to you.

A relationship does not just happen. It passes in a predictable manner through phases of development. Each phase is unique and special in the development and life of the relationship, as you will learn shortly. Allow the relationships in your life to work for you rather than against you. Not only will your loneliness diminish, but you will discover a new self-confidence, strength, and realistic well-being growing within you.

2

It's Your Choice

How did I ever get myself into this? I kept thinking as I guided our van over the highway toward the retreat center. My family and I would be spending the next week there.

Several months earlier when I had not been so busy I had agreed to lead daily seminars at this family retreat. Although I tried to blame my frustration on my already-too-busy schedule, more truthfully my discontent was apprehension in disguise for the unknown I would be facing during the coming days. It was a role I wasn't used to, one whose demands I wasn't sure I could meet.

My personal fears finally became audible as I muttered the refrain circling in my mind, "How did I ever get myself into this?"

"But Dad, didn't you agree to lead the seminar sessions for the week?" asked Stephen, overhearing my negative comment. "You did have a choice, didn't you?" he innocently inquired.

"Yes, Stephen, I did," I had to reply, realizing that he was correct. It had been my choice.

The warm sunlight began to break through the branches of the tall Norway pines as we emerged from the woods onto a grassy area where two rows of cars were

EVERYBODY NEEDS SOMEBODY SOMETIME

parked. I pulled the van alongside the cars, and we all piled out. Lugging suitcases, sleeping bags, and fishing poles, we made our way up the hill to the registration booth. Situated outside under the shade of a large oak tree was a table with a huge welcome sign over it. Three staff persons eagerly awaited each new arrival.

"Welcome!" greeted one of the enthusiastic staffers as a happy-face nametag was pinned on each of us. "Wear these at all times so everyone will know who you are." Just then a very pleasant, kind-looking man walked up to introduce himself.

"Hello, I'm Steve Walton, the retreat director," he said as he warmly shook my hand. I introduced the family and thanked him for all the helpful materials he had sent me in preparation for the week. He told me how pleased he was that I was able to be with them, and his warmth and sincerity were encouraging. I was already feeling better about being there.

We made our way along the path toward our assigned cabin, and I soon spotted it nestled under the pines. The sign over the door read, "Spruce." Trying to think of something nice to say, both my wife, Judy, and I realized that it would take every bit of creative talent we had to transform this stark, concrete-floored cabin, furnished with twelve single bunk beds, one table, and two chairs, into "home" for the week. Ordinarily these cabins were used to house groups of boys or girls, not families.

The courtyard bell clanged, announcing that the orientation meeting was about to begin. This would be the first gathering of our entire group. Once inside the meeting room, I looked around noticing the overly polite people cautiously finding places to sit. After a brief greeting, the

IT'S YOUR CHOICE

retreat staff reviewed the schedules, rules, and program for the week. No one, including myself, seemed to be listening very closely, being far more interested in each other than in the program being presented.

Everyone in the room seemed to be strangers, both to me and to each other. Then my eyes caught a familiar face over in the corner of the room. It was Jack. He and his wife, Beth, had seen me in counseling several years before. They said therapy had helped, but I never had felt totally comfortable about their decision to discontinue. In any case, I had grown to care deeply about both of them. Now I felt a sense of personal comfort in seeing Jack and knowing there was at least one person here whom I knew.

Jack was sitting alone with his children. Where was Beth? My eyes finally caught his, and I gave him a big smile. He returned my gesture with a brief nod and then quickly looked away. My sense of personal comfort left as quickly as it had come. I wondered if his marriage was faltering and if he felt uncomfortable about my being here. *Maybe I'm being overly sensitive,* I thought.

My attention was drawn back to the front of the room as the director, Steve, asked everyone to introduce himself to the group. Interest was immediately stimulated as, beginning with the front row, the introductions began. A middle-aged woman stood and said, "I'm Connie. I hope I will be accepted here; I realize most of you are married and have children." After a long pause, she continued, "I am divorced and live alone. Quite honestly, I have been so lonely lately that I just had to find a way to be around some people in a more personal way. You see, the only folks I routinely see are the two women I work with and my next door neighbor in the apartment building." Al-

EVERYBODY NEEDS SOMEBODY SOMETIME

though there was no outward response from the group, I knew she was speaking not only for herself but for many others.

A quiet, unassuming man slowly stood and introduced himself, his wife, and their little girl. "My name is Warren," he began, "and this is my wife, LuAnn, and our daughter, Karen." At that moment Karen made her own introduction with a sudden outburst that totally drowned out Warren's words. His face turned red, and he couldn't decide whether to continue standing or to sit down. With relief he watched LuAnn produce a bottle of milk from a bag nearby and pop it into Karen's screaming mouth. There was an immediate welcomed silence.

It appeared that Warren had something more he wanted to say. After another pause, he stumbled through an explanation of how his life had changed in the past year. He had terminated a career in teaching to become a youth worker for a Christian organization that reaches out primarily to hard-core delinquent kids.

There was another uncomfortable lull. "It's not going so well," he faltered. "In the next few weeks I will have to make some big decisions about continuing in this youth ministry. I hope you folks can help me." Quickly he sat down.

I was deeply and somewhat curiously moved by the way he appeared so shy and uncomfortable yet could be so honest about himself with this group of total strangers. I found myself wanting to get to know Warren better.

The exercise continued as individuals stood, gave their names, and told a little about themselves and their lives. Near the front a man of small stature, who seemed to have an unusual amount of energy, rose. "I don't know

IT'S YOUR CHOICE

what I'm doing here," he blurted out. Immediately his wife retorted, "Don't worry, I do." Everyone laughed nervously, not knowing what to expect next.

"My name is Dan and this, as you can already tell, is my wife, Sherry." Dan proceeded to tell us that he really should be at home tending to his new job, which often required sixty hours of work each week. His need to talk seemed to take over as he went on and on about how this job was for him the "chance of a lifetime." His overly busy life was further manifested in his being chairman of his church. That very evening he was missing his first church meeting in over four years. "You should be honored," he said with a smile. With that comment Sherry tugged on his shirt sleeve and reminded him that this was one time when he didn't have to take charge. He sat down.

A tall, very distinguished-looking man stood next, exuding self-confidence and poise with every word and gesture. "My name is Henry, and I work for the State Department of the United States Government," he announced in a clear, precise voice. Henry explained that his being here was really a matter of chance as he was in transit between assignments. He had just completed two years in Denmark and was now on his way to Australia. Somewhat subtly he made reference to being under a great deal of pressure and looking forward to the week to rest and sort out some decisions of his own.

Moving on to the back of the room, behind several additional rows of people, a soft, gentle voice spoke out, "I am Lisa. My husband, Paul, is here too; but he decided to walk down along the lake until after this meeting." She quietly continued, "He doesn't like crowds."

There was something about Lisa that intrigued me, but

EVERYBODY NEEDS SOMEBODY SOMETIME

at the moment I wasn't sure what it was. She spoke in a very unassuming manner, but her message was strong. It wasn't what she said, or even how she said it—there was something more. On the surface she was quiet and shy, but deep inside she seemed to have much to give to the people in her life. Her openness, like Warren's, did not seem compatible with her shy personality. I was looking forward to meeting Paul.

We had finally worked our way to Jack, who was sitting in the back corner. With a burst of enthusiasm he stood to introduce himself and his children. In a pep talk fashion he said he knew this was going to be a great week for everyone. I didn't want to be skeptical of the strength of his feelings, but the suddenness of his zeal didn't match with the indifference written over his face throughout the entire meeting. I began to recall that Jack had been skillful at keeping people at arm's length, and this kind of enthusiasm was one of the ways he succeeded in doing it. Furthermore, he gave no explanation for the absence of his wife, Beth.

After several more people introduced themselves, the meeting was dismissed with the instruction that we all meet again in two hours at the dining hall for dinner. A special meal was planned for our first night. Stepping outside, I felt the warm afternoon sun hit my face. I thought, "Great, I've got a couple hours with the family to relax and enjoy this beautiful place." Walking toward our cabin, I started to unwind from the meeting and the long drive earlier in the day.

Through the trees, my eyes were drawn to a woman running up the path toward us. It was Beth. I hadn't seen her for years, but she hadn't changed. She was crying.

IT'S YOUR CHOICE

Embarrassed as she drew closer, she tried to wipe away the tears.

"Beth, what's wrong?" I asked. "Where are you going?"

Between sobs she tried to reply, "I–I don't know, but I ca–can't stop now."

I extended my arm across her path, risking that she would push it aside and continue on. Instead, to my surprise, she hung onto it as she started to sob and cry even harder. My family had tactfully gone on ahead, most likely to spend the next two hours without me. This, we learned, would be the pattern throughout the week.

I suggested to Beth that we walk together, hoping that some conversation could eventually get started. As we made our way down through the woods to the waterfront, the peacefulness of nature all around us seemed to have a calming effect.

"Do you care to talk about it?" I inquired.

"It's too much!" she replied.

"What's too much?" I asked, puzzled.

"I can't bear the thought of an entire week with Jack. Having all this time alone, just with each other, is more than I can handle."

As we continued talking, I learned how Beth and Jack had established a comfortable distance in their marriage relationship, effectively using the business, children, a busy church schedule, and several other outside interests to keep them from each other. For both of them the kind of intimacy that this week was offering *was* just too much. For one week those barriers of isolation had been taken away, and the thought of it was overwhelming Beth. My guess was that Jack was facing the same predicament.

I was reminded just how frightening intimacy can be if

EVERYBODY NEEDS SOMEBODY SOMETIME

you are not accustomed to having it in your life. While others at the retreat were most likely concealing similar fears, Beth was "letting it all hang out." Even though the setting was ideal for a peaceful week, and everything had been planned to provide Beth and the others with a pleasant retreat experience, her response to it was panic.

Searching my mind for some good immediate advice to help her, I discovered I didn't have any. Yet, she was much calmer.

"Thanks, this has really helped," she said with relief.

I was surprised. "What helped? I haven't really given you any answers."

"But you were here when I needed someone," she explained. "Just before we met on the path, in my tears and confusion, I had asked God to make Himself real to me in my moment of uncertainty. The next thing I knew you had extended your arm to me. That's how you helped," she said with a big smile.

How often God uses human contact to lead a person to Him again! It is not *what* we do, but rather our presence which is a balm to a person in pain.

"What should I do?" Beth inquired. "I really feel like I don't want to be here."

My mind flashed back to the similar feelings I had experienced during our trip earlier that day. Drawing on the counsel of my eleven-year-old son, I said, "But Beth, you did make the choice to come, didn't you?"

"Well yes, I did. But I didn't know how I would feel after I arrived! Maybe I could sign up for several special projects, which would allow plenty of time for Jack to try out his new boat, alone." She was desperately searching for a way to get through this week with as little pain as possible.

IT'S YOUR CHOICE

"But aren't you falling back into old patterns if you do that?" I reminded her. Reluctantly, she had to agree.

We talked about how she could make several choices for this week. Her first choice had, of course, already been made. She was here. Now what remained was how she would choose to spend her time and what kind of attitude she would have in doing it. Reassuring her of God's continual love for her and promising my human support during the coming week, I challenged her to build a new level of intimacy with Jack.

With hope in her eyes, Beth smiled and disappeared up the path through the woods. Again alone, I walked on down the shoreline, hoping to get a look at some of the sailboats available for our use. It had been at least a couple of years since I'd enjoyed a good sail. My thoughts were diverted, however, as I spotted Jack passionately wiping down one of the most beautiful inboard speedboats I have ever laid eyes on. From a distance, unnoticed by Jack, I paused and watched him work with care and patience as he prepared to launch his boat. I thought how good it would be if his and Beth's relationship could receive the same kind of cherished care.

I decided to make my presence known, so I walked over to Jack and said, "This is one beautiful boat. It looks new."

"Just got it this spring," replied Jack not looking up from the piece of chrome he was polishing.

The enthusiasm Jack had shown at the meeting was now totally gone. He made no effort to conceal his frustration as he put all his energy into that little piece of spotless chrome.

"I talked to Beth," I said cautiously. There was silence

EVERYBODY NEEDS SOMEBODY SOMETIME

as Jack kept rubbing. "Jack, I'm sorry it's so hard," I continued.

Throwing his polishing cloth to the ground, Jack retorted, "I am too!" and walked away.

I decided not to follow him, but rather to walk on alone back toward the cabin. My personal frustrations about being at the camp had vanished as I became involved in the needs of those around me. Jack and Beth were just one couple of many who were frustrated in their marital relationship.

As I walked, my mind started going in circles, trying to figure out the tangled human truths behind the calm exterior of the camp. The setting was beautiful. The grounds and staff were fully prepared to give everyone a pleasant, restful week. Even the weather was cooperating. Youth workers had developed an all-day program for the children, even removing that responsibility from the parents.

Why did I sense tension and restlessness throughout the group? Was it the same reason that Beth and Jack were resisting this restful, uninterrupted situation that had been created for them? The answers to all these questions seemed to point to the personal relationships of these people. Many of them were strangers to their spouses and to God. As long as they could hide behind busy schedules and obligations outside of these relationships, they could tolerate the emptiness. But when these barriers were removed and intimacy was encouraged, they couldn't handle it.

Each individual who came to the retreat center that week brought unique tensions from troubled relationships. Many were struggling with their marriages, others

IT'S YOUR CHOICE

with jobs, some with friends; and others were just plain lonely. In addition, they now were forced to relate to people they had never met before.

How powerful are relationships in our lives? The state of our current relationships and our ability to form new ones are directly related to how we feel about ourselves and others. By this time I was convinced that most of the people at this retreat needed help. My work was cut out for me.

Just as it was both my choice and theirs to be there that week, each of us chooses our relationships. Even when we feel that we are forced into some of them, we choose whether or not we are going to maintain them. We reach out to certain people. We respond to others who reach out to us. The choice of each of these couples to attend the camp could be the door, I decided, by which I could help them recognize their need for good relationships and their ability to consciously mold them.

The people at the retreat were in many ways no different from people everywhere. Each of us has experienced relationships that produce anxiety or insecurity or that have ceased to grow or to function properly. But such relationships can be improved, and new relationships need not begin to suffer if they are properly understood and handled. Again, it's your choice.

You may have realized that the people at the retreat were professing Christians, yet their problems and struggles were just as real and painful as those experienced by people outside the church. Christians are not exempt from life's pressures. Their relationships, even with other Christians, often suffer.

EVERYBODY NEEDS SOMEBODY SOMETIME

Near the end of the book, I will let you in on what happened during the retreat to the relationships mentioned in this chapter. But now let's turn to the typical problems plaguing relationships and to the practical aspects of their day-to-day development.

3

Popular People With No Friends

Startled out of a sound sleep by the ringing of the telephone, I tried to focus my eyes on our bedroom clock while reaching for the receiver. It was nearly an hour earlier than my usual rising time.

"Hello," I mumbled.

"Hello, Jerry? This is Bill. I hope I didn't wake you," he replied.

"You did, but it isn't the first time," I retorted. My mind flashed back to when we served together on a governing board and had frequent early morning meetings.

"I need to talk to you," Bill continued.

"Fine, how soon?" I asked.

"Tonight will be soon enough," he announced. After proceeding to tell me he would be over at 7:30 P.M., he hung up.

Now more fully awake, I tried to comprehend what had just taken place. Going through the conversation in my mind, I realized he hadn't asked to come over—he had *told* me he was coming.

Throughout the day my mind kept recalling that early morning call and Bill's unusual persistence about getting together. He had offered no reason for our meeting,

EVERYBODY NEEDS SOMEBODY SOMETIME

though it was obviously important to him. The day passed quickly, and at exactly 7:30 Bill's car pulled into the driveway.

Bill was currently chairman of an organization in which I had also been active. We had become acquainted at the meetings a couple of years ago. He quickly got to the point and told me that the organization was in serious difficulty. Morale was low. Programs were stifled. One by one he listed the problems that constantly were plaguing him. None of the other board members could talk effectively enough to each other to help straighten things out.

"After tossing and turning all night, I racked my brain trying to think of someone with whom I could talk," Bill continued. "Then early this morning, I thought of you, because of how well we communicated when we worked together two years ago."

Together we were able to come up with some ways to improve the problem situations in the organization. But the longer we talked, the more I realized that he didn't want just answers. What he really craved was my listening ear and understanding.

Further on in our conversation Bill started talking more and more about himself. He talked about some career options. Next he went into family problems with which he had to deal. Finally he got right down to the basic issue.

He was lonely.

At first this realization totally stunned me. Bill was one of the most popular people I knew. His chairmanship was the result of a popular vote by the members. At every party, Bill was predictably in the middle of the action. Whenever we walked together through the corridors of

POPULAR PEOPLE WITH NO FRIENDS

his large office building, everyone spoke to him and he always had an appropriate reply. Bill was friendly, talented, and full of the charisma that attracts others. Yet as we conversed, the realization came clearly to both of us. Outside of his family, he had no true friends.

Bill continued, "What really upset me last night was when I tried to think of someone to talk with. My mind drew a blank. I had to face the fact that I had no one."

"I'm really pleased you called. Only next time don't make it quite so early in the morning," I said with a grin.

While helping him on with his coat, I suggested that we get together again. He readily agreed and pinned me down to a time one week later.

Bill left a different person. He was relieved, and his sense of humor had returned. His situation had not changed; the burdens of the organization were still awaiting him. Nevertheless, something special had happened. Bill had checked me out and discovered he had a friend.

INVISIBLE LONELINESS

I had always thought that people fall into two basic categories: lonely people and people with friends. Now I realize that there is a third type: popular people with no friends. These people are usually very active, living out their lives constantly in the presence of others. They know a large number of people and *are known* by an even greater number. Yet they have no true friends.

These individuals spend their time attracting people and being attracted by others. Nothing deeper than superficial contact is ever made. For them that connecting

EVERYBODY NEEDS SOMEBODY SOMETIME

link called the relationship just does not exist. The development of attraction with other people is as close as they have allowed others to come. Surprisingly, they often talk of intimacy and closeness, but they never really manifest it in their lives.

Where do you belong? Are you obviously lonely? Do you have a circle of friends that will stand by you no matter what? Or, are you in that third category, being a popular person with no friends? Do you have many acquaintances but no deeply committed relationships? I am convinced that most people today fall into this third group. Bill was one of them. Outside of his family, he had no one. And as is so often the case, he was not aware of it until the night before our visit when he desperately felt the need to talk with someone.

Similarly, you may go along ignoring that nagging loneliness by continuing to do what you have learned to do so well. You keep busy! You stay active! You don't give yourself a spare moment to think of your loneliness and the people whose acquaintances you value. How often have you sincerely said to someone you wished you had more time together? Yet seldom do you fulfill that wish.

If your schedule is full enough and you can maintain sufficient demands on your time, you will usually convince yourself that you are not lonely. Your numerous contacts with people will maintain the *illusion* that you have many friends. But when the going gets rough, how many people do you know who will take the time out of *their* busy schedules to listen to you? And how many of them would you want to know about your personal problems? Answer these questions and get a reading on the true status of your relationships.

POPULAR PEOPLE WITH NO FRIENDS

Who would you turn to if your spouse died?
What person would you ask for help if you lost your job?
Who would you call on if you needed to discuss a serious personal problem?

Arriving at an answer to these questions will quickly help you evaluate your personal standing with friends. When you are busy and things are going well, people surround you in what I call "pseudo friendships." These people create an image of caring concern, but most of them will not come through with an emotional commitment or a listening ear. These acquaintances will fail you for various reasons (or with various excuses) but the result is the same: In a time of crisis, pseudo-friends will not fill your emptiness.

YOU ARE NOT COMPLETE ALONE

Contrary to the teaching of many psychologists, you cannot be complete within yourself. The discovery of yourself and fulfillment of your needs come only when you are linked together with others in committed relationships. Alone, with ourselves as the only reason for actions, we can never feel totally worthwhile. Rather, these feelings are acquired as we give and receive from others.

Our strength comes in a similar fashion through the bonds of our relationships. Ideally, our first taste of such strength comes from a relationship with God through a personal commitment to Him. Knowing the power of this truly committed relationship, we can more openly and confidently enter into intimate human relationships.

EVERYBODY NEEDS SOMEBODY SOMETIME

Sometimes we commit ourselves to others first, and thereby gain a strength that helps us trust God more fully. If you discover that you have a loneliness which has been camouflaged behind a busy schedule and counterfeit friendships, let me show you how to change this by teaching you how to build lasting, committed relationships.

RELATIONSHIPS AND TREATMENT

Dr. William Glasser states in his book *Reality Therapy*, "At the time any person comes for psychiatric help he is lacking the most critical factor for fulfilling his needs, a person whom he genuinely cares about and who he feels genuinely cares about him."[1] Whatever emotional problem that person is experiencing, the absence of relationships is a critical factor.

His advice extends to the counselor as well. "The therapist," he states, "must be able to become emotionally involved with each patient. To some extent he must be affected by the patient and his problems and even suffer with him. The therapist who can work with seriously irresponsible people and not be affected by their suffering will never become sufficiently involved to do successful therapy."[2] I have found that this is the very core of what makes people get better.

Why is this true? Why is the relationship so important in treating emotional illness? The answer is self-evident. *Emotional problems and the loss of relationships often go hand in hand.* The problems continue until basic emotional needs are met. These needs cannot be met without

POPULAR PEOPLE WITH NO FRIENDS

relationships—that natural, life-giving process of caring and being cared for. Over and over again, I have experienced the thrill of seeing life return to the eyes of extremely depressed people when they can once again experience involvement in a personal relationship. Therapy—a relationship with a therapist—is the threshold of this process. However, this relationship must lead to other relationships so that eventually therapy is no longer necessary as other commitments take over.

Recently a woman announced in one of my therapy groups that this would be her final session. She felt restored and whole again. Her anxiety and depression were gone. Clinically speaking, her therapy had been successful. One of the group members asked her what it was that helped her get better.

"Just being here," she explained. "Feeling understood and knowing that you folks cared was essential. Then I was able to reach out to some of you in this same manner. Your caring, coupled with the awareness that I was needed by you, restored my self-confidence. I now realize that I must always belong to someone, somewhere. Everyone needs people, and the group helped steer me back in that direction."

Routinely I ask people who are "graduating" from group therapy this same question: "What made you better?" Each says it in his own way, but the answer is the same. Health is restored by the sense of belonging that comes from the entire experience of being part of a group.

Although clinics such as ours have taken the group method and made it an effective treatment tool, it certainly is not limited to treatment. We all need these experiences and the relationships that provide them.

EVERYBODY NEEDS SOMEBODY SOMETIME

NO TWO RELATIONSHIPS ARE THE SAME

Each relationship is unique. While many may seem similar, no two are exactly alike. Each one needs to be treated individually, taking into consideration its special traits and characteristics. Some are casual associations, while others are more serious. Some have to do with work, others are for fun. There are relationships that become deep and intimate, while others appropriately remain more superficial. We choose to cultivate some relationships, while we learn to accept others.

No relationship should be taken for granted or considered static. If your expectations become fixed, they can force people into roles that are foreign to them. There are times when people masquerade, not being themselves in a relationship, because of the image either they want to project or that others push on them. Let me illustrate.

A friend of mine and I are frequently at the same social gatherings. His usual behavior is outgoing, gregarious, and witty. People actually wait for him to arrive to stimulate the action; he is known as the "life of the party." But occasionally he arrives in a more serious mood. Persistently the others push him into his usual role. In recent months, however, we have seen less and less of him at our social gatherings. One day I asked him where he had been keeping himself. I was shocked when in total honesty he said he really didn't enjoy being with the group. I couldn't believe it! He went on to explain that more often than not he preferred being serious and passive, but he felt he could not be accepted that way by our group.

"Whenever I told them that nothing was wrong, that I just felt like being quiet, they wouldn't believe me," he explained.

POPULAR PEOPLE WITH NO FRIENDS

As a result, he has withdrawn from the group. Let me emphasize that *not allowing a person to be himself in a relationship is a form of rejection* in disguise.

Just as people live out their lives, relationships, in a similar fashion, pass through phases. They are born, live out their lifetime, and come to an end. Some relationships have short, full lives; others last longer. A number of relationships end abruptly, the premature ending being like a sudden death. This is often the situation when a father receives a business transfer and moves his family to another city. These are among the relationships that take unexpected turns; however, under normal conditions most relationships follow a predictable pattern.

THE FIVE PHASES OF YOUR RELATIONSHIPS

Each phase of a relationship is unique and logically follows the other. There are five phases in all: *attraction, testing, commitment, maintenance, ending.* Look at each one in summary form.

1. *Attraction*

Attraction is the initial phase. Here two people find themselves drawn to each other as if by an invisible magnet. Attraction is the first indication of a potential relationship. In one sense it is the beginning. Strong positive emotions are often experienced in this phase. If, initially, two persons are forced together against their will, an attraction must be formed before the development can go to the next phase. Let me make clear that a relationship does not exist with just an attraction.

EVERYBODY NEEDS SOMEBODY SOMETIME

2. *Testing*

During testing you seriously check out the potential of developing a relationship. In the process of testing you are also being tested. During testing, a relationship begins to take a structure, a form, as you explore each other's personality and needs. Pressure is put on that structure as you spend more time together and learn to depend on each other. You begin to believe in the other person and that person believes in you. Testing is a process of gradual mutual acceptance that can be one of the most stressful phases of the entire development of a relationship. During this phase, you continue to ask yourself if your needs will be met from this relationship and if *you* are willing to meet the needs of the other person. Furthermore, it is a very tenuous time because a commitment has not yet been made.

3. *Commitment*

By mutual commitment the relationship comes into being. In the first two phases, signposts leading to a relationship exist; but the relationship itself is not real until there is commitment. Promises, both actual and implied, are made in this phase; they seal the commitment.

Limits are set and a definition is given to the relationship. Your extent of commitment determines the level of intimacy you will have. Certain relationships require a narrow and defined commitment since you enter some relationships for a specific purpose. Others, such as marriage or a close friendship, will involve a deeper, more intimate commitment. Remember, there is a place for all types of commitment, depending upon the unique nature of the relationship.

4. *Maintenance*

The hallmark of a lasting relationship is service. Serving one another puts the commitment into action. As you care for one another in this manner, the relationship grows strong. This phase essentially involves living out the relationship. Relationships are maintained by the experiences that go on within them. They can be very dynamic, changing from one day to the next. At times the preceding phases will be called back into active service to assist in maintaining the relationship. Maintenance is usually the longest phase, for it is the adulthood of the relationship.

5. *Ending*

Many of our personal relationships eventually come to an end. However, there are some exceptions. We can have an eternal relationship with God and fellow believers. "For God so loved the world that he gave his only Son, that whoever believes in him should not perish but have *eternal* life."[3] Other relationships last until one of the persons involved dies. But most relationships end after a given period of time. They can end haphazardly—or skillfully, with sensitivity and forethought. It's up to you. The manner in which you end it is as important as what occurred in the relationship itself.

These phases are a part of virtually all relationships,

and they make their appearance in the above order. Each phase enters much as each actor does in an unfolding drama. Attraction is exciting, giving immediate interest to the possibility of a relationship. Testing cannot take place unless this attraction is present. Similarly, testing is in preparation for the next phase, commitment. Each phase adds meaning to the next and must not be underrated or ignored. A common mistake, for instance, is to try to live out the relationship in the maintenance phase without the security of commitment. No healthy relationship can be built this way.

As the drama continues, each phase, following its initial appearance, fades into the background as the other phases make their entrance. The earlier phases usually continue to function in lesser roles but may be called back to center stage from time to time to offer their services. For example, if a relationship becomes boring or commonplace, attraction may return to bring life back onto the scene. Also, if confusion were to evolve, testing and commitment may need to make further appearances. This is often the case in marital relationships as couples go through various stressful experiences. Therefore, as the relationship grows and phases make renewed appearances, the marriage becomes fuller and more complex.

Although people often prefer to ignore the ending phase, it too takes its place on the stage. Ending is one of the most influential of all phases, for often it determines the lasting memory of the entire relationship.

By knowing these phases and what occurs in each, you will be able to understand more fully your relationships and how they affect your life. So now let's look at each phase more carefully.

4
Phase 1: Attraction

There is an immediate attraction. The room is crowded with people, but this person stands out above the others. The two of you strike up a conversation, and the attraction grows. You "click." As if sharing a newly discovered treasure, you want all your other friends to meet this person. You are excited about your new association.

Following the initial encounter, you continue to relive each detail. Already you are contriving ways the two of you can get together again. Any affirming gesture on your new acquaintance's part brings a faster than usual response from you. Something is happening, and you are excited.

What I have just described is the attraction experience. Everyone at some time or another experiences it. The feelings and process are the same. All you have to do is substitute your specific details. I realize that all attractions are not this dramatic. Yet in varying degrees this is the general process. You have become keenly aware of another person and are especially interested in how you are viewed by him or her.

Attraction hails the beginning of a possible relationship. The development of anything new charges the air with excitement. Change is happening in your life. Because attraction is merely a beginning, the future is still uncertain. Mystery still shrouds the initial phase in the development of any relationship, and most of us respond to the challenge and the newness with heightened activity and expectation.

Let me emphasize here that the attraction is not always an immediate reaction. There are times when it comes slowly. How often have we heard good friends confess that when they first met they didn't care for each other at all? In other words they are saying that they needed to know more about one another before the magnetism began to draw them together.

Whether the attraction occurs early in the formation of a relationship or later in that process, it must take place or there will not be a relationship. When you find that a person is initially unattractive to you, a discovery of some attractive aspect must ensue before the relationship will continue to unfold.

WHAT CREATES THE ATTRACTION?

What is it that brings about an attraction? What elements create that human magnetism toward another? Everyone *knows* when it is happening, but few people really understand *why*. When you sense an attraction, most likely a combination of the following major elements are present.

Physical Appearance

The first exchange two people have when they meet is usually not verbal but visual. It is physical appearance that first arouses your interest.

PHASE 1: ATTRACTION

One day a friend attended a class with me as my guest. Following the session, he made his way to a person on the other side of the room and began a conversation. When I asked him later if he knew that person, he replied that he didn't. The person just looked like the type he would have something in common with.

In the area of physical appearance, oftentimes sexual attraction is considered. (I will address this subject more fully later in the chapter.) However, one who is comfortable with one's sexuality is usually considered attractive to others. Now don't miss my point. The attraction is not the result of a person's sexual emphasis, but rather is caused by comfortable attitudes toward himself and others.

Specifics are important here—grooming, cleanliness, and posture are all important. Most of my clientele are conservative Midwesterners. Sometimes as new patients enter my office and see me for the first time, they sigh with relief. They proceed to say how happy they are that I am not a bearded therapist with beads. My suit and tie bring an initial acceptance. Yet, I am also aware that in another setting, a beard and beads might perform that same function for a different group. In any case, remember that your physical appearance speaks loudly and is usually your first message.

Openness

As soon as you start talking with this new person in your life, you will get a reading on his or her openness. Eye contact is a main indicator. Is this person comfortable when the two of you look at each other? An open person radiates warmth and, with refreshing freedom, expresses what he or she feels and thinks. The person is accepting of

EVERYBODY NEEDS SOMEBODY SOMETIME

you, not wanting to control; yet very interested in what is important to you.

One day as I was seeing patients in a rural medical clinic where I routinely consult, a farm couple was referred for marriage counseling. Their family doctor warned me that this would be "a challenge." He said nothing more but wished me luck as I entered the office for my first consultation with them. Only moments later I knew exactly what my doctor-friend had meant. The husband began a monologue. He covered all his wife's faults and praised himself for how hard he worked. He made it clear to me that I had better "fix his wife" so their marriage could get back on the right track.

After half the session had lapsed, I literally had to shout to get him to be quiet so his wife could say her first words. This man violated every principle for building a good marriage. He also did a good job of initially turning off people so they would never bother to get to know him. At the end of our first session, I was fascinated by my response. I liked him! There was an attraction. What was it?

It wasn't his appearance. He wore the same clothes he had done chores in that morning, and the barn odor accompanied him. I didn't share his beliefs. But . . . he was open! I found his honesty refreshing. I did not like what he said, yet I knew exactly where he stood.

Openness creates attraction because it expresses trust. Honest interaction is not phony or confused by messages with double meanings. In contrast the defensive person is unattractive. Covering up the true message or saying only a portion of it is a backhanded form of rejection. By withholding fragments of his message, he is displaying distrust and nonacceptance of the other person.

PHASE 1: ATTRACTION

I realize there is value in withholding parts of yourself from the other person until you can determine whether a relationship is developing. There are also appropriate and inappropriate times to be open. The person who often "sticks his foot in his mouth" is one who is unskilled in choosing the appropriate time to send a message.

In any case, when you sense an attraction toward someone, most likely they are being open with you.

Similarities

Everyone values his personal interests, hobbies, beliefs, and experiences. Therefore when you meet someone with similar likes and dislikes, attraction is immediately stimulated. How often two people at a social gathering go off to a corner to discuss hunting, fishing, theology, children, or whatever interest they share in common.

This aspect of attraction is not immediate but comes to pass as two people get to know each other. Sometimes a skillful host or hostess may start the process at a party by introducing two people and pointing out their common ground. When you experience attraction to someone, most likely the two of you have similar interests.

Curiosity

Curiosity plays an important part in some attractions. This feeling comes into play when someone says, "I would like to meet that person to find out what he is really like." Curiosity is not usually an initial attraction element; rather it joins other elements to strengthen your desire to get to know someone. Often it is aroused by an interest

EVERYBODY NEEDS SOMEBODY SOMETIME

you may hope to share with someone else. At other times it is just plain curiosity. It is this force that entices crowds to gather for a chance to catch a glimpse of a celebrity rushing past.

Acceptance

Acceptance is a powerful part of any growing attraction. Actually it is always involved in the other attraction elements, but is important enough to consider separately as well. Everyone wants to be liked. In one way or another we all seek approval, and acceptance satisfies this concern within us. We all need our sense of personal value and worth supported by another person's opinion. When someone shows a warm personal interest in us, there is an immediate attraction.

One prerequisite needs to be mentioned here. There are times when a person is starved for acceptance and has suffered several rejections. When sincere acceptance comes, the initial response may be caution and suspicion. If the acceptance is maintained in a sincere, consistent manner, the suspicion will diminish as true attraction emerges.

It is easy to identify the power of acceptance in your attraction to someone. Whenever individuals are contemplating joining a church, the friendly acceptance of the congregation is a strong factor in bringing them to a decision. The neighbor you are the closest to is often the one who welcomed you into the neighborhood with a cake or a hot dish on moving day.

Judy and I routinely welcome newcomers into our neighborhood with a plate of homemade rolls and a personal visit. Last summer one of our new neighbors about a

PHASE 1: ATTRACTION

half block away was badly cut by his lawn mower. His wife sent one of their children, not to the next door neighbor, but all the way down the street to our house for help. Our *only* previous contact with this family had been our visit months earlier. We had shown acceptance and they had felt attraction.

What it all comes down to is, *you are usually attracted to someone who is attracted to you.*

ATTRACTION DEFINED

To truly understand attraction, you should not focus too much of your attention on the person to whom you are attracted. All the elements we have just looked at are important for bringing about an attraction, but they are not the attraction itself.

You are attracted to someone not primarily for what they are, but rather for what you become as a result of your contact with them. The most significant happening is not with them, but with you. They are merely the catalyst.

When you are experiencing an attraction and are being drawn to that other person, pause to glance at yourself. A part of you is being awakened as you learn more about yourself through this association. It is the exciting transformation taking place within yourself that creates the attraction you feel toward the other person.

Jesus' first encounter with Levi, the tax collector, keenly illustrates this process of change when attraction is present.

> Later on as Jesus left the town he saw a tax collector—with the usual reputation for cheating—sitting at a tax collection

EVERYBODY NEEDS SOMEBODY SOMETIME

booth. The man's name was Levi. Jesus said to him, "Come and be one of my disciples!" So Levi left everything, sprang up and went with him. Soon Levi held a reception in his home with Jesus as the guest of honor. Many of Levi's fellow tax collectors and other guests were there.[1]

Levi met Jesus. Without any apparent reservations Jesus invited him to come and be one of His disciples. Jesus reached out to him, *as he was,* and an immediate attraction was created in Levi. A change had begun. A man who loved money and material wealth immediately sprang up and left it all. Levi realized he wanted to be what Jesus knew and accepted he could be.

THE "HONEYMOON PERIOD"

Oftentimes in the development of a new relationship there is a strong, lingering attraction. This creates an unrealistic situation in which the good aspects of a relationship are strongly emphasized while the objectionable side or differences are overlooked. In jobs, political offices, and other new relationships where strong demands will be made immediately on you, this "honeymoon period" often exists only for a short while. For the president of the United States, for instance, unconditional acceptance usually lasts about one hundred days. As time goes by, this period of blind approval will diminish regardless of the kind of relationship. This change can occur either gradually or abruptly, but recognize that this is a natural process as the relationship continues to develop. You are moving through the phases toward "maintenance."

Initially the vanishing honeymoon period may be con-

PHASE 1: ATTRACTION

strued as rejection or loss of commitment by one or both parties. Yet it is really a form of acceptance. You are now one of us, part of the family, and there is no longer any reason to give you special treatment. Attraction continues to act as a magnet, but it takes on a different form. Mature respect, earned from time and service together and coupled with continued interest, serves to create a much firmer base for the relationship than the initial untested response.

Some attractions turn into counterfeit relationships. You may be convinced that you have a strong relationship with someone when in reality you have not progressed beyond a mutually strong attraction for each other. Romantically, this is known as infatuation. Attractions are exciting and significant as they lead you toward potential relationships, but don't be misled. That is all they do. Attraction is only the first phase in the development of a relationship. *A relationship does not exist until there is a commitment.*

RED FLAG ATTRACTIONS

Not all attractions are beneficial. The confusing part is that all attractions *feel* good, otherwise they wouldn't exist. Persons involved in objectionable situations often have neglected to recognize honestly the kind of attraction they initially experienced. Attraction that suggests immediate gratification for a stiff price later on is what I term a *red flag attraction,* indicating "Stop. Don't continue to get involved." Following are some questions to help you determine the healthiness of your attractions.

EVERYBODY NEEDS SOMEBODY SOMETIME

They aren't designed to make you run from relationships, but rather to identify, understand, and be aware of where attractions are leading you.

1. Does this attraction seriously conflict with other commitments? Certain friends, hobbies, jobs, and other situations attracting your attention may appear very good in themselves. But when you evaluate their effect on your other committed relationships, their actual destructiveness becomes obvious. An extramarital affair fits perfectly into this group as a red flag attraction. In itself it appears as a warm friendship. But by placing it beside your committed relationship of marriage and parenthood, it looks entirely different: It is destructive.

2. Is the attraction moving you towards vital commitment or a stalemate? Not all relationships require total commitments. But they do require some kind of verbal understanding as to each individual's status. If your attraction for someone is not inspiring trust or reliance, check out the reason with the other person. If he or she can't tell you why the association isn't moving toward commitment, strongly consider relinquishing it. This is one of the most confusing and emotionally draining situations in which one can find oneself. My advice is either to get the attraction moving toward commitment or drop it.

3. Is the attraction morally wrong? This third question is similar to the first. I identify it separately because it is easy to dispute the first question convincingly when you are determined to hold on to the red flag attraction. For the Christian this question places the attraction squarely against the standards of God's Word. If the attraction is sin, get rid of it. Identify, understand, and be fully aware

PHASE 1: ATTRACTION

of where your attractions are leading you. Then with God's guidance make your choice either to stay with them or to let them go.

THE PLACE OF SEXUAL ATTRACTION

Where does sexual attraction fit into relationships? In any discussion regarding attraction, sexual response is oftentimes mentioned first. Undoubtedly, sexual attraction is a primary force in romantic relationships.

Initially sexual attractiveness seems very important because it is often the first element that draws you toward someone in a budding romance. As the first conscious element of attraction in the developing relationship, its importance is often overemphasized. Don't be misguided here, but understand where the true source of strength in sexual attraction lies. Yes, the physical side is strong, but not by itself. True strength in sexual attraction comes only as it combines with other nonsexual qualities that can be grouped together under the term "*agape* love."

The whole spirit of *agape* love is to give, expecting nothing in return. Joy comes through giving. As this spirit of selfless giving is combined with your sexuality, you achieve a true sexual attraction as God designed it to be experienced in the marriage relationship. The romantic relationship is not totally sexual, but the sexual element makes it uniquely romantic. The proper place for the sexual element was designed by God to be in the attraction phase of romantic relationships leading lovers to marry.

EVERYBODY NEEDS SOMEBODY SOMETIME

WHAT DO YOU DO WHEN A RELATIONSHIP MUST BE DEVELOPED AND THERE IS NO ATTRACTION?

If an attraction does not exist, you must create one before the relationship will truly develop. Rather than merely trying to seek a trait within that person upon which to kindle an attraction, ask yourself what obstacles are blocking the attraction or getting in the way of your liking that person? If the answers do not readily come, you will most likely find them by taking the following steps.

Listening

When someone gives you his full and undivided attention, it is natural to respond positively. People need others to be truly interested in them. One very basic way of demonstrating this is by listening. Although it is significant to hear verbal messages, of greater importance is your ability to reveal successfully that you are listening.

Listen to more than words. Listen with your eyes by picking up facial expressions, body language, gestures, and other nonverbal messages. The use of eye contact creates a form of intimacy. By giving affirmative nods you are sending positive signals of acceptance to the other person, vividly demonstrating interest and acceptance.

Also learn to listen with your feelings. Ask yourself, "What am I feeling?" as the person is speaking. Your intuitive sense is an accurate receptor of important messages.

Lastly, demonstrate your sensitivity to the other person by responding to an unspoken message. Several times a

PHASE 1: ATTRACTION

day in the counseling session I will pass the Kleenex box when someone starts crying. Also you might endeavor to put into words the mood you are perceiving in the other person. For example, you could say, "You look sad as you talk about it. This must be difficult for you." Responses such as these tell people you are genuinely trying to understand. This leads to the next tool—understanding.

Understanding

Everyone wants to be understood. A frequent plea that accompanies the disclosure of feelings or ideas is, "Please try to understand." Some people just naturally attract others. My mother-in-law is one. For several years she worked as secretary to the president of a small Baptist college in Ohio. One of the things she did best was never written into her job description. She was the friend and counselor to a steady flow of students and faculty who came to her office each day. What made her so attractive to this wide variety of people? She *understood*.

There are many times when she did not agree with what she heard, but that was not important. She has that special ability to put herself in the other person's place, thereby creating a sense within the other person of being understood.

Too often, understanding and agreement are considered one and the same. This is wrong and confusing. Understanding does not always mean agreeing. You can understand or desire to understand without compromising your personal viewpoint, which may be entirely opposite. If you are having little success in understanding a message,

EVERYBODY NEEDS SOMEBODY SOMETIME

simply stating that you *want* to understand will be enough to create the attraction.

Need

The third tool helping to create attraction is need. Relationships are built on meeting needs, and one of the strongest elements for creating attraction is for the other person to feel needed by you. When you can convincingly express this need that they can meet, an attraction will begin. Being needed gives an individual a sense of worthiness and elicits a positive response. Create a need, and an attraction will be present.

Likemindedness

Likemindedness is the fourth tool, and I regard it as an optional one. When you can successfully listen, understand, and create within the other person a sense of being needed, an attraction will definitely be present. Likemindedness is not essential for attraction. We can all think of close relationships which thrive on differences and the freedom to debate them. However, sharing ideals, values, and goals makes attraction become stronger. In order to foster attraction, seek areas in which you can agree and begin building on them.

The apostle Paul's missionary journey to Athens is a beautiful illustration of how this tool functions. Paul was visiting one of the cultural and educational centers of the world. He was about to address a crowd of philosophers and scholars with vastly different ideas about religion from his own. In that particular part of the world many

PHASE 1: ATTRACTION

gods were believed to rule, while in his message of Christianity Paul was about to tell them that there was only one true God. He needed to create an attraction. How did he begin? Let's look at the account:

> Men of Athens, I notice that you are very religious, for as I was out walking I saw your many altars, and one of them had this inscription on it—"To the Unknown God." You have been worshiping him without knowing who he is, and now I wish to tell you about him.[2]

Tactfully, Paul found a common ground of agreement with the group and from there delivered his sermon. The attraction came first, as he displayed an acceptance of them and their altar to the unknown God.

Attraction, the first actor on stage, has now finished the opening scene, one filled with excitement and anticipation. A new relationship is beginning to unfold, and in turn you are discovering new aspects of yourself. It's an awakening.

5

Phase 2: Testing

"Does she really like me?"
"Will I be hired?"
"Can we become friends?"

When you begin asking these types of questions, you are in the *testing* phase of a relationship. The *attraction* has already been recognized. There is no doubt in your mind that you have an interest in a relationship with that person. However, even at this point the relationship is still more of a wish than a reality. You like what you have experienced thus far and are hopeful that it will continue to develop into a committed relationship.

THE TESTING PHASE

What are some of the signposts to look for in the testing phase? How do you know you should press on toward a committed relationship? Obviously, the specific answers to these questions vary with every relationship. Below are general guidelines you can follow, but let me caution you here that in each relationship you must apply them personally. Although another person's advice can be help-

PHASE 2: TESTING

ful, you must make the choice to develop or not to develop a relationship.

Will Your Needs Be Met?

Relationships are formed and maintained when needs are being met. During the *testing* phase (this will reverse later) you must ask what your real needs and expectations from the relationship are. For example, when considering a job, you would obviously consider the financial arrangements. But in addition, you would appraise the potential satisfaction from the job and the people with whom you would be working each day. Frequently I hear someone say that his job doesn't pay much but that the work is interesting and the people are great. Consider your needs and whether this relationship will meet them.

Availability

Will the person you are interested in be there when you need him? Availability is mostly a question of a person's free choice, something that will be discussed more fully under commitment. Then there are those situational factors such as schedules, distance, and other commitments that hinder one's availability in a relationship. When contact with a person seems sporadic because of unavailability, you may not wish to press on towards commitment. Someone you don't see often would find it hard to fulfill the needs of a committed relationship, and before you come to rely on them, the testing phase of the relationship should give you the choice to refuse involvement.

EVERYBODY NEEDS SOMEBODY SOMETIME

Ability to Adjust

Adjustment is that fundamental thread that runs through all relationships. The life of any relationship is directly connected to the persons' abilities to adjust to one another. Interwoven with your ability is your willingness to adjust. These two very different parts of adjustment often get confused as being one and the same.

Frequently in the marriage relationship, one spouse accuses the other of not being willing to adjust, when in reality they are *unable* to make the changes the spouse is requesting. The willingness is there, but the ability is not. For instance, a husband may be willing to help out with cooking, but his lack of experience may make him unable to cook a good meal without considerable instruction. Or a wife may seem unrealistically optimistic at times to her husband, but she truly may find her natural optimism nearly impossible to squelch.

Adjustment involves recognizing what the other person needs and making the changes within yourself to meet those needs. When adjustment comes easily, the relationship is dynamic and strong. In contrast, when adjustment is restrained, a relationship will often wither and die.

Willingness to Commit

People often "talk a good line," thus stimulating attraction in the other person—but the commitment never occurs. Willingness to make a commitment must be determined; otherwise there will not be a relationship. You will just keep talking about "someday" having one. One of you may fear getting too close or be reluctant to pay the cost of commitment. This willingness (or lack

PHASE 2: TESTING

thereof) to give of yourself must be worked out during the testing phase before you can go on.

THE DRAMA OF TESTING

Testing is a phase of frequent intrigue. While living out the drama of testing, we often experience extreme emotion, from the heights of ecstasy to the depths of despondency. A constant struggle evolves to separate what is factual about this potential relationship from what is purely emotional.

Television viewers experience the testing phase daily in the all-American soap opera. The producers of these addicting programs have captured the power of emotions generated in the process of testing potential relationships. Day after day the audience is held spellbound by the perpetual drama of one tale of testing leading into another.

"Does John still love Mary?"

"Will George be promoted by his superior?"

"Can Sue and Carol ever really be friends?"

In voices dripping with charisma and intrigue, these questions are temptingly asked at the close of the program's episodes with the familiar, "Tune in tomorrow to find out." And thousands do!

The ongoing success of these never-ending sagas manifests the fact that people relate to these situations as if they are intimate parts of their own lives. The emotions the dramas evoke run parallel to similar ones in real life, and many people feel emotionally drained after each episode. Most likely when you experience emotional ten-

EVERYBODY NEEDS SOMEBODY SOMETIME

sion, you are in the testing phase with someone in your life. In a sense, you are experiencing your own soap opera—but one of real people following their own needs rather than scripts.

Similar to attraction, testing remains somewhat quietly in the background while other phases make their appearances. Although testing follows attraction in the sequential development of a relationship, this phase, like attraction, can often reappear as the relationship continues to grow. Testing will almost always reappear whenever a committed relationship seems to be in question. However, in some relationships testing is rarely heard from after its initial appearance. It is in the less stable relationships that testing continually recurs. Only the solidification of the relationship will make the reliance upon repeated tests unnecessary.

THE TWO FORCES IN TESTING

Why is testing so often emotionally charged and complex for the persons involved? What creates the intrigue? The answers to these questions involve the dynamic interplay between the people developing a personal relationship—usually neither is in control or feels assured they know the other's feelings. While you are testing a person to determine whether you want to enter into a relationship, you are also being tested by them in the same manner. Accepting the other person is only part of the process—your part. You must also be accepted by him or her. At this point nothing is definite while you each wait for the other's response.

PHASE 2: TESTING

This period of uncertainty is often an emotionally charged part of the developing relationship. Impatiently wanting to speed along the process, you may be overly accepting early in the testing phase. However, when the other person is slow to respond, you may awkwardly retreat to a safer, less committed position. Then there are other times when you hold back your acceptance, watching for the other person to move first. This waiting game can result in a stalemate that will either deter or end the relationship. Take a risk. Be open. You can get the relationship moving toward commitment—or else you will learn the relationship is not for you. Let's look at some situations that reflect the pressures and risks typically experienced during the testing phase.

THE DATING RELATIONSHIP

Children are often the best teachers of basic lessons about life. They are involved in the same interplay of forces as are adults when a relationship is developing, but they have not yet erected a sophisticated system of defenses to conceal what is happening. This was the case as I observed a budding young romance in our neighborhood.

Trying not to appear too nosy, yet seeing the obvious interest Jim had in Donna, I had to ask, "Do you know if Donna likes you?"

"I don't know yet, for sure," he replied. "I've got to talk to Paul first."

"Why Paul?" I inquired.

"Because Paul is going to ask Mary, who will check with Liz, Donna's best friend, to find out for me."

Lost somewhere between Paul and Liz, I decided to drop

EVERYBODY NEEDS SOMEBODY SOMETIME

the subject for the time being. Later in the day, our conversation resumed when I noticed Jim's happy countenance.

"Did you get the word?" I asked.

"I sure did. Donna told Liz that she could let Mary tell Paul that she 'kinda liked me—if I liked her.'"

For Jim and Donna the testing phase was taking great strides forward. Not only was it moving along, but its progress seemed to involve every kid in the neighborhood.

Remember, you did the same sort of thing in the early days of your life. Sensing the risks, you protected yourself by going through as many different people as possible to determine if that special person had an interest in you. Are you aware now, years later, that nothing has really changed? You are still indirectly trying to protect yourself. Only now the process has become more sophisticated.

For example, what about the lunch date you have with that strategic person in your department? Even though you don't want to show your interest obviously, sometime during the get-together you hope the conversation will gravitate to your real concern. Does he or she know if you're being considered for a promotion?

Let's face it, we all do it.

THE JOB OFFER

He sat in my office puffing on his pipe, totally preoccupied with his own thoughts. Dutifully his wife tried to speak for both of them as she reported the progress in their marriage during the past month.

PHASE 2: TESTING

Glancing over at her husband, she smiled and said, "He has been this way for over a week now!" Continuing to speak for him, she explained that he was anxiously waiting to hear whether he was accepted for a promotion that would associate him with an exciting group of executives in the company. Realizing that the marriage did not need to be discussed any further, I decided to go with the obvious subject on their minds.

With my casual reference to the promotion, he snapped on like a switch. For the next thirty minutes, nonstop, he outlined every detail, challenge, and reward that he would experience in the new position. For the first time in a career of staff positions, he would become the director of a department, supervising more than twenty employees. Instead of assisting with routine programs within the company, he would be creating new ones.

He went on to tell me how he had never been aware of his keen interest in creating new programs in marketing—a talent that he hoped would now be utilized. With a smile of pride written all over his face, he said he would have parking privileges in the executive garage and access to the V.I.P. lounge.

Then as quickly as the smile came, it disappeared.

"I'm really scared!" he said.

"Scared of the responsibility?" I inquired.

"No, scared that I won't get the job." With a deep sigh, he continued, "I don't know what I'll do if I'm turned down."

I told him I could understand how he could be disappointed and let down if that happened. But why should he be afraid? I reminded him that there was really nothing

EVERYBODY NEEDS SOMEBODY SOMETIME

to fear. He still had his present job. His income was secure. His home and family were strong. Actually nothing would change for the worse.

"No, you are wrong!" he emphatically interrupted. "Whether I get this promotion or not, things will never be the same after this."

As I continued to listen, this young would-be executive taught me a lesson about the testing phase that I will always remember. Being accepted by the other party in a relationship with this potential *does* cause permanent change within you. You will never be the same. Let me explain further.

REJECTION: THE GREATEST RISK IN TESTING

"Get angry!
"Disagree!
"Do almost anything!
"Just don't leave me!"

In all my years of counseling, I have learned that the source of most fears is rejection. Nobody wants to be turned down.

The concept of rejection is often accompanied by honest-to-goodness fear. Why? During the testing phase a decision of acceptance or rejection must eventually be made. Mutual acceptance allows the relationship to become definite and move on to the next phase, commitment. On the other hand, when a relationship with you is rejected by the other person, your hopes for that relationship crumble around you. Excited anticipation is replaced by despondency and often self-doubt. It is no longer possi-

PHASE 2: TESTING

ble to avoid feelings and thoughts of undesirability. With this loss of self-confidence, a feeling of hopelessness creates a belief that you are incapable of pulling yourself out of this state.

(Rejection is not limited to the testing phase. I introduce it here because this is where it is first experienced in the development of your personal relationships. As a matter of fact, the further you progress in the phases of a relationship the more acutely you will feel rejection if it occurs.)

After you experience rejection, the prospect of establishing the relationship usually ends. Thus your plans for the future will alter. However, not *everything* ends. Some of these "endings" are really beginnings. Let me explain.

Recall the attraction phase of one of your relationships: the hopes, interests, and potentials within you that were awakened and brought to your awareness. Recollect the sense of excitement and aliveness you felt as you discovered them.

The young would-be executive I talked to was awakened to a strong desire to supervise his own department. He knew he could do it if given the opportunity. His creativity was stimulated as he envisioned the new programs he could develop while working alongside several men whom he admired. If he were denied the position, those desired potential relationships would never be born; *yet the awakened awareness of these new interests and talents would remain alive within him.*

Frustrations come with the realization that you cannot immediately utilize newly discovered resources. A new restlessness is created, fueled by a lack of fulfillment as you try to reconcile yourself to the status quo. The young

EVERYBODY NEEDS SOMEBODY SOMETIME

aspiring executive said he would never again feel the same about his present job. With the awareness of new available opportunities, satisfaction in the stability of the present state of your affairs evaporates.

When this happens to you, persevere. Hang in there! Keep trying! It is often the agony of rejections that precedes the ecstacy of success. The apostle Paul knew rejection well. He was stoned, whipped, thrown into prison, and shipwrecked. But *he did not quit.* Some relationships ended, but *he* continued. He fought the good fight, he finished the race, and there was a crown of righteousness laid up for him in heaven.[1]

When you experience rejection, limit your view of it to that individual relationship. Don't take the stance of being a "rejected one." Learn from that experience and go on.

Your situation is not as hopeless as you may think. Yes, you have been rejected by a person and denied a relationship. However, you retain control over the newly discovered potential and abilities in yourself. They belong to you. They have not rejected you. Take comfort in that realization and do not withdraw.

Instead, take these newly awakened resources and seek other relationships where you can use them. Perhaps you will look for new employment opportunities, seek new friendships, or align yourself with another group. Use your rejection as a springboard to new relationships rather than as an excuse to withdraw from trying again.

For many people the key to their present success is directly related to the manner in which they handled previous rejections. Let me repeat. When you experience rejection, take what you have learned about yourself from

PHASE 2: TESTING

the attraction and testing of that experience and *seek new and often better relationships.*

BEYOND TESTING

Some persons never move past the testing phase in their associations. If you find that you are confused and uncertain as to a relationship you have with someone, and it has gone on this way for a long time, most likely you are locked into a state of continuous testing. You may think you have a relationship, but no commitment exists. Face the testing phase directly and allow it to do its work, but once you have your answer either move away from the association or move on toward true commitment.

Now the testing phase has fully entered the stage of the developing relationship. You will learn in the next chapter that commitment takes on many levels. Some are total while others are more limited and definitive.

6
Phase 3: Commitment

Crowds were pouring into the auditorium, and everyone was excited. A drone of voices filled the air from the hundreds already in their seats. Rumor had spread throughout the district that Lance Martin was a candidate, but tonight it would become official.

A flurry of activity on the platform occurred as technicians adjusted lights and strategically positioned the television cameras in front of the podium. What appeared to be miles of electrical cord lay on the floor, making the equipment that was to relay this event to the outside world operable.

In the wings Lance stood huddled with his aids, conferring on last minute strategy. Reporters were trying to get through unsuccessfully. Lance was nervous, though his insecurity was concealed beneath his broad smile and confident tone of voice. Running for political office was a new experience for him, and he knew he needed help—the kind of help that Charlie could give him.

"Five minutes until air time, Mr. Martin," came the cue from a fellow with a clipboard as he hurried back to one of the cameras.

PHASE 3: COMMITMENT

"Thank you," Martin quietly replied.

His mind drifted back several weeks to a meeting at his client's home. It was a cold evening in February, and he hadn't known what the meeting was all about. He had agreed to go because he highly respected his client, who was also a good friend. Arriving precisely at the hour suggested, he was greeted at the door and quickly ushered to a library. Once there, he was introduced to a group of folks he quickly recognized as leaders of his political party.

Everyone seemed to know each other, except for one man sitting over in a corner. Like Lance, Charlie was a newcomer who possessed special talents in dealing with the current problems of the district. After introductions, they got right to the point.

"Lance, our party is in serious trouble," commented the self-appointed chairman.

"Our district needs new leadership," said another.

"We need your help," stated Lance's client.

"What kind of help?" Lance asked.

"We want you to be our candidate for the legislature," was the response.

Thinking back to that evening, Lance recalled that it was Charlie who had convinced him to give up his job in private life for a few years to help their troubled district. Charlie was the one who could do such convincing. He had a power of persuasion that was unsurpassed. But Charlie hadn't committed himself to the campaign team. That had created a big void, causing Lance to question privately his effectiveness in handling the awesome task that he was undertaking.

EVERYBODY NEEDS SOMEBODY SOMETIME

Lance and Charlie had talked several times since that first evening. In addition to all the data and insight Charlie had provided the prospective candidate, he and Lance seemed to have that special chemistry between them that brought out the best in each other. In spite of all the support and information, however, Charlie still hadn't committed himself to working with Lance.

The problem was this: Several weeks earlier Charlie had received an attractive job offer; if he accepted, he would be on an airplane heading for California at exactly the same time Lance announced his candidacy. Just when Lance Martin felt he needed a friend the most, Charlie was flying across the continent. *How could this happen to me?* Lance was thinking. No one had heard from Charlie since he learned of the job offer.

"Three minutes until air time," came the familiar cue. This brought Lance back to the present. His make-up received last minute touches. A fine perspiration that had started to form on his upper lip was lightly blotted.

"This is your moment, Mr. Legislator" came a send-off from one of the excited aids. They all huddled together in the wings, watching their candidate as he was escorted to center stage. He took his position behind the podium, and a tiny microphone was clamped to his lapel. With a slight smile he thought to himself, *I wonder if anyone can tell this is my first telecast.*

A hush fell over the audience as the assisting attendants disappeared. Now Lance stood alone with two television cameras directed at him. "Remember, the camera with the red light on is the one that's picking you up. Be sure to look directly into it," instructed the fellow with the clipboard. Lance's heart started to pound. He felt

PHASE 3: COMMITMENT

perspiration beading on his face. The heat from the flood lights was stifling.

A cue card displaying "45 seconds" was held up. Anxiety started to build. His mouth was dry. Clearing his throat, Lance tried to fix his opening statement firmly in his mind. Momentarily his mind flashed back to his childhood, when he had been forced to play in his first piano recital. *I've got to pull myself together,* Lance thought as he glanced toward the wings searching for reassurance from his aids.

Then it happened! Entering the studio and standing front and center was Charlie. His big smile and thumbs-up gesture signified to Lance that he had turned down the new job offer, cancelled his flight to California, and was committed to helping with the campaign. A new surge of strength ran through Lance as his anxiety vanished. The red light on the television camera flashed on brightly, and he was on the air.

"Ladies and gentlemen, tonight our district stands in serious trouble. Solving critical problems demands new leadership. In response to concerned citizens like yourselves from throughout this district, I am proud to announce my candidacy...."

From that moment on, there was new stamina in Lance Martin that carried him successfully through his campaign and on into public office. As Lance later related this story, he pointed out to me that it was Charlie's *commitment* at that precise moment that unleashed the power of self-assurance within him. The smile and thumbs-up gesture that evening just before the telecast sealed their relationship and freed Lance to go on into the campaign with the strength and confidence he needed.

EVERYBODY NEEDS SOMEBODY SOMETIME

THEN THE RELATIONSHIP REALLY STARTS

When commitment occurs, your relationship becomes a reality. The magnetism of the attraction phase has worked. The testing has been successful. Now your commitment to one another seals the relationship.

Commitment is a powerful phase—perhaps the most powerful. In the development of a relationship the commitment must be clearly understood by each person involved. Distrust and disillusionment all too often result from misinterpretation and false assumptions about a commitment that really does not exist.

Your commitment creates the base for the relationship. Its permanence is directly attributable to the personal commitment of each individual to the other. Not only does commitment inject power into a relationship, but it also unleashes new strength within the individuals themselves. It takes a good relationship to bring out the best in almost any individual. Charlie's commitment to Lance the evening of the telecast, for instance, helped him to display confidence and conviction.

Successful businessmen understand this principle and practice it in operating their companies. The president of a local corporation reminded me of this as we discussed the phenomenal growth of his business during the past few years. He stated that the ultimate strength of any company, including his, is not in the assets, sales, market, or product. Those are all important, but a business is people—the people who work with a mutual commitment to the company's success. In them lies a company's true growth potential.

Relationships need commitment because it spells secu-

PHASE 3: COMMITMENT

rity for the persons involved. After the uncertainties of testing, a relationship finally is born. Commitment confirms that you are attractive and desirable to the other person. All the aspects about yourself that you had hoped were acceptable definitely are. As a result, commitment reinforces your self-esteem and strengthens your self-confidence. It is always easier to accept yourself when you know that others have accepted you. The fear is removed that almost everyone lives with in varying degrees during the testing phase. With the commitment *you are accepted*.

Once the fear of rejection is removed, some amazing changes occur as people let go and become themselves. They can show both their good and bad sides without fear that the other person will walk away. After all, the mark of good friends is that they can tell each other almost anything and know that it will not destroy their relationship. The commitment remains strong, keeping the friendship vitally alive.

Once the commitment has been established, you are free to get on with the purpose of the relationship. I have found in marriage counseling, for example, that very little improvement can be made until there is some kind of commitment. A husband and wife who remain committed to their marriage vows, who do not see divorce as an option, progress more quickly. However, when a commitment to the marriage is not clear, I try to get the couple to make a short-term commitment to the therapy relationship. Then *some* security is established. They at least know that regardless of what happens within their marriage during this time, they will not leave each other.

This same principle is true in other relationships as

EVERYBODY NEEDS SOMEBODY SOMETIME

well. When an employee continues to question whether he should remain in a job, his productivity is limited. We all know people who limp along in their jobs, always talking about leaving but never doing so. The absence of commitment on their part makes the relationship weak.

Commitment is a conscious act of the will. You decide to what extent you will give of yourself and your time to the other person. Commitment gives definition to a relationship.

It is important to recognize that you have far more conscious control in this phase than you have had in the two previous phases. While going through attraction and testing, you often experienced a sense of vulnerability. At one point you felt accepted and thought the relationship was underway. A few days later the relationship seemed to be falling apart in front of you. Vacillation is common during the first two phases. When you consciously make a commitment, the relationship becomes solid. Feelings coalesce, giving direction to the relationship.

... AND SAY IT!

Silent commitment by one person is not enough; commitment must be communicated, and preferably reciprocated, or the relationship will flounder as though there were no commitment at all.

When you are ready to make your commitment, *say it*.
"I will be there."
"I will do it."
"Yes, Sir, you can count on me."
Short simple statements, such as these, said in sincer-

PHASE 3: COMMITMENT

ity, are all it takes to put the commitment into action. But it must be stated.

To remain strong in your relationship, you must continue to be aware of the commitment you made during this phase. From time to time the commitment needs to be restated. This consideration keeps people from questioning the relationship.

"Nothing has changed."

"I am with you all the way."

"We need you more than ever."

Statements of this type keep your commitment working at top efficiency. Yet there are also times when your actions speak the commitment better than words. Charlie's commitment to Lance was said without a word. His presence at the right time, a broad smile, and his thumbs-up gesture expressed it eloquently.

THE COMMITMENT PROMISE

A promise is always something very special. In the Scriptures, the word "covenant" is often used concerning a promissory agreement. There is unique meaning to a promise both for the one making it and the one receiving it.

Remember as a child how you would require a promise from a friend before you would share a special secret. "Promise not to tell?" always preceded the passing on of special information. Promises have a vital place in relationships as well. A broken promise is one of the worst tragedies between persons.

A commitment is basically a decision involving a promise. *It's your word.* You promise to give of yourself to someone for the good of the relationship you share. Sometimes this promise can be limited or defined for a relationship with a specific purpose. Here you may be required to give only a part of yourself. At the other extreme, a promise may be very broad, and you will give totally of yourself. Such a promise is found in good friendships or in marriage.

Your commitment promise, or covenant, covers three major areas. Each stands alone, yet is related to the other two areas. The level of commitment encompassed in these three elements is guided by the amount of yourself you choose to give to the other person. Let's look at each of these areas.

Exclusiveness

This involves placing your relationship in its proper location on your list of priorities. The other person in the relationship should then be informed of the rating. In the marriage commitment the promise of total exclusiveness is stated in the vows: "... forsaking all others."[1] However, all relationships do not require this kind of commitment; the level of exclusiveness in them should be based upon needs and purposes.

For instance, a social worker was hired by our clinic primarily to coordinate a special group therapy program. The clinic supported the program on the condition that she lead the sessions each week. Prior to accepting this position, she stated that she would not be available after 2:30 P.M. each day. Her family came ahead of her outside job, and she believed it was important to be home when

PHASE 3: COMMITMENT

her children arrived from school. The limits to her employment commitment were clearly defined.

Frequently she refused other requests for her time during the middle of the day because they conflicted with the group session. Eventually, however, it became necessary to move the group session to a time later in the afternoon. The clinic knew they would lose this social worker, because she had clearly defined the limits of her commitment to the program before she was hired. With the change in the group's schedule, she had to resign, yet she did not break her commitment promise.

You are the one who must determine the level of commitment you will make in each of your personal relationships. A lesser commitment is not necessarily wrong if it is explained at the beginning *before* the relationship gets underway. Problems occur when a deeper commitment is implied than is carried out.

When you do not define your level of commitment, the other person will do it for you. It may be nice of him to help you in this way, but all too often there is a problem. He usually commits you more than you choose to be. When you find yourself asking *How did I get myself into this?* more than likely you let the other individual define your commitment for you. Set your own limits. You can do it best.

Conditions

The conditions under which the relationship will exist are set in the commitment promise. Generally, the fewer the conditions, the greater the commitment. A strong commitment is one without conditions such as the marriage relationship, in which the ultimate commitment removes all conditions "... for better, for worse."[2] Conversely, a greater number of conditions usually reflects a lesser commitment.

To form strong relationships, keep conditions to a minimum. The absence of conditions allows greater flexibility for the individuals to be themselves. Each person then has room to make mistakes and to change his mind.

Most relationships in our lives, however, are limited. These are formed to serve a specific purpose, such as: a student and his professor, an employee and his boss, and a member on a committee. In all these situations, conditions help rather than restrict the relationship. Such limited relationships become strong through a careful definition of the conditions. The student/professor relationship is maintained by a clear-cut explanation of the assignments. The employer/employee association functions best with a definite job description. Each committee member works more efficiently when the goals and purposes of the committee are well-defined.

Duration

This part of the commitment promise defines how long the relationship will last. Most relationships are for a limited amount of time, even though people approach them believing they will last forever. Students have relationships with each other as long as they are enrolled in school. Employees have a relationship as long as they remain with that company. Christians meeting at a retreat center have a very special relationship, but its duration is limited to the time of the retreat.

PHASE 3: COMMITMENT

Marriages, families, and very close friendships all tend to fall into the lifetime relationship category. Yet even some of these relationships go through major changes and essentially end as you once knew them. Part of the stress within families today involves the inability of some members to accept changing relationships as the siblings grow up and move away from home.

When you know the duration of the relationship at the beginning, make it clear in your commitment. Here again, vague, open-ended relationships often restrict rather than free. Knowing how long the relationship will last lets you move about more freely without fear of a premature ending.

Thinking back to the story at the beginning of this chapter, Charlie promised Lance that he would work with him throughout the campaign. No matter how tough things got, Lance knew Charlie would be there. Charlie also knew that once the election was over, his commitment had been kept and he was free to leave.

As couples join my therapy groups, they face this question head-on. Meeting with each other week after week, discussing personal aspects of their lives, they quickly create a natural intimacy among themselves. Soon they begin asking about the duration of these newly formed relationships.

"Will we ever see you folks after we leave the group?" they often ask.

I usually jump in to explain that they probably will not. I don't discourage friendships continuing from the group, but the nature of the relationships and their commitment usually don't carry over into social relationships.

The rapid development of closeness is stimulated by the

EVERYBODY NEEDS SOMEBODY SOMETIME

fact that these couples meet weekly for an hour and a half at the clinic for the purpose of resolving problems within their marital relationships. Although members of the group experience freedom within their new relationships, many conditions structure their time together. When each couple is better, they will leave the group with all its intimacy. At that time the relationship and commitment to the other couples will probably end.

THE SEARCH FOR FREEDOM AND INTIMACY

We cannot leave the subject of commitment without taking a moment to look at two conditions everyone seems to want and need.

"Man, I'm not committing myself to anybody or anything. I'm going to be free to do my own thing."

"I want to really be close to someone, somewhere. I need the intimacy that comes when you are free to come and go as you choose within a relationship. Any relationship without that freedom is really a box that I don't want to find myself in."

In one form or another, I hear these statements over and over again from persons who are searching for *freedom* and *intimacy*. The paradox is that most individuals are running from a commitment—yet, it is this very commitment that gives them the freedom and intimacy for which they are searching. Commitment is often erroneously perceived as restrictive, tying people down or putting them in boxes. Stop and take a good look. You will find that commitment does not block intimacy and freedom but provides a setting in which both *will* grow.

PHASE 3: COMMITMENT

Our happiness and well-being are tied to our relationships and what we experience within them. The fear of rejection causes us to withhold our intimacy and lose our sense of freedom. In self-defense we imagine we will find freedom by avoiding relationships and the hassles that oftentimes accompany them.

On the contrary, you will find freedom when you have a relationship without fear of rejection, a relationship whose commitment is firm. Likewise intimacy, that sense of being very close, is discovered through this same process.

Don't abandon commitment in search of these two elusive treasures. Rather find them through your commitment. Commit and be free to be yourself within your relationships. Commit and discover the security and joy of being truly open.

When the commitment is there, you are safe to be totally open—or naked, as the Bible states it—without fear or embarrassment. "And the man and wife were both naked, and were not ashamed."[3]

7

Phase 4: Maintenance

What does it take to maintain a relationship?

What makes some relationships work better than others?

How is authority established within a relationship?

These are the questions we must answer to understand how to live out our relationships to their fullest. We have experienced the attraction. We have gone through the testing. Our commitments have been made, bringing the relationship to a solid reality. Now, how do we maintain it?

It is tempting at this point to list the usual "how to do it" tools of a good "relationship maintainer." Even though tools and techniques are important, they are insufficient in themselves to answer our questions fully. How often have you said that there must be more to it than methods? There *is* something more.

OUR HIGHEST IDEAL IN MAINTAINING RELATIONSHIPS

The key to maintaining your relationships is *service*. You serve one another. Throughout the Scriptures, we

PHASE 4: MAINTENANCE

hear this instruction again and again. Don't worry, though; what follows is not just another lecture on caring for one another as our Christian duty.

Such caring is, of course, necessary; but our preoccupation with what we have heard many times should not blind us to the range of truths this instruction implies. Service goes much deeper and is far more powerful than most of us realize. Scripture says it best, so let's look at a few of the many passages throughout God's Word that instruct us in this way.

> For, dear brothers, you have been given freedom: not freedom to do wrong, but freedom to love and *serve* each other. For the whole Law can be summed up in this one command: "Love others as you love yourself"[1]

There it is. We are free, not to run off and do our own thing, but to stay and serve. Our commitment paves the way. No matter how many different ways we may try to say it, the lesson is summed up in six words: *Love others as you love yourself.*

Let's go on.

> Slaves, obey your masters; be eager to give them your very best. *Serve* them as you would Christ. Don't work hard only when your master is watching and then shirk when he isn't looking; work hard and with gladness all the time, as though working for Christ, doing the will of God with all your hearts. Remember, the Lord will pay you for each good thing you do, whether you are slave or free. And you slave owners must treat your slaves right, just as I have told them to treat you. Don't keep threatening them; remember, you yourselves are slaves to Christ; you have the same Master they do, and he has no favorites.[2]

EVERYBODY NEEDS SOMEBODY SOMETIME

Let's not be distracted here by the issue of slave versus free. At the time the apostle Paul wrote this epistle, one half of all the people in the Roman Empire were slaves. Paul chose to use a very familiar relationship to teach the lesson of serving one another. Slaves were to serve their masters with gladness. But the slave owners were instructed to treat their slaves in the same manner, "as I have told them to treat you."

The lesson is clear. *Service works in both directions.* Slaves serve masters—masters serve slaves. We serve each other as slaves, for we all have the same impartial Master. By now, you may be thinking that you have heard all this before. You probably have, but now be sure you haven't been misinterpreting these verses you've heard so often. They are not instructions to become doormats or to be "yes men" to each other. Rather we are to "encourage each other to build each other up, just as you are already doing."[3]

We all need encouragement. (If you don't, I'd like to meet you.) Encouragement comes from outside of ourselves. It is not self-praise but requires the hearts and voices of others besides ourselves. We serve by encouraging and building up one another. The "you" in the above verse is singular. Paul was not asking one group of people to support another. Rather, the encouragement he requested was a one-to-one process. Each person was to individually serve another.

Now let's take this concept of service as our highest ideal and examine how Jesus lived it out in His life. In His example we can begin to see the true meaning of the lesson God has for us. Here the power and authority from practicing service become apparent.

PHASE 4: MAINTENANCE

> Jesus told them, "In this world the kings and great men order their slaves around, and the slaves have no choice but to like it! But among you, the one who *serves* you best will be your leader. Out in the world the master sits at the table and is served by his servants. But not here! *For I am your servant.*"[4]

Jesus Christ, our King of Kings, holds the standard for us to follow. Although the apostle Paul in Ephesians tells us that we are slaves to Christ, here Jesus declares that He is our servant. This apparent contradiction spells out how service can be the highest ideal of all relationships, even including our relationship with Jesus Christ, the Son of God. Although He is our Master, He is our Servant. *Service travels both ways.*

Not only did Jesus tell His disciples that He was their servant, but He showed them.

> ...And how he loved his disciples! So he got up from the supper table, took off his robe, wrapped a towel around his loins, poured water into a basin, and began to wash the disciples' feet and to wipe them with the towel he had around him.[5]

In the humblest of ways, He washed their feet. Note that He removed His robe and "wrapped a towel around his loins." The lowliest slaves dressed this way when they served their masters. Imagine yourself girded with a towel, kneeling down to wash the feet of those whom you love. What a demonstration of humble service!

Where does all this lead? What is the result of this service one to another? The following passage serves as an excellent summary.

> Then make me truly happy by loving each other and agreeing wholeheartedly with each other, working together with one

EVERYBODY NEEDS SOMEBODY SOMETIME

heart and mind and purpose. Don't be selfish; don't live to make a good impression on others. Be humble, thinking of others as better than yourself. Don't just think about your own affairs, but be interested in others, too, and in what they are doing. Your attitude should be the kind that was shown us by Jesus Christ, who, though he was God, did not demand and cling to his rights as God, but laid aside his mighty power and glory, taking the disguise of a slave and becoming like men. And he humbled himself even further, going so far as actually to die a criminal's death on a cross.

Yet it was because of this that God raised him up to the heights of heaven and gave him a name which is above every other name, that at the name of Jesus every knee shall bow in heaven and on earth and under the earth, and every tongue shall confess that Jesus Christ is Lord, to the glory of God the Father.[6]

Study this passage carefully. Within these verses, the entire lesson of service as God's highest ideal for our relationships is systematically laid out. Our service is evidence of our love. We are to love and work together in unity. Jesus set the example by becoming as a slave and dying "a criminal's death on a cross" for our sins.

But the lesson does not end at this point. Christ was then raised to be King of Kings and Lord of Lords. Jesus' service as evidence of His love for us led God to raise Him to His supreme authority. One is the result of the other. From His actions we learn that *true authority is not self-imposed but springs from your service to, not your demand from, the people over whom you have authority.* Placing the needs of the other person in a relationship before your own may look like passive subjugation, but it is actually the key by which healthy relationships are maintained and by which true authority is established.

Let me tell you about three different individuals who

PHASE 4: MAINTENANCE

have this authority—an authority they acquired from the service they so generously gave to others.

The first is a medical doctor whom I have known for years. Everyone for miles around comes to him for medical care, and absolutely everyone in the county knows and respects him. Despite the fact that he is a general practitioner, no one in the community would consider going to a medical specialist without receiving his recommendation first. His word is final, considered authoritative by the entire community.

One day during lunch together, we talked about the respect his patients have for him. He is a humble man and expresses some apprehension over the total confidence that his patients place in him. He said that living in a small community and being out of medical school for many years has made it difficult for him to keep current on new developments in health care. Therefore he knows it isn't his credentials or superb abilities as a doctor that give him authority. Instead, the authority and respect he receives from his patients, he is convinced, come from two factors. "First, my patients are aware that I genuinely care about them. Second, I am there whenever they need me." Stated in another way, he has authority because he *serves*.

My next example of a person with authority is in an entirely different context. She is a secretary to the president of a growing company. The success of the business has elevated her boss to a highly respected position in the business community. While managing the growing company, the president faces heavy pressures and decisions daily.

His secretary is excellent at her work. She also has an intuitive sense that tells her what her boss needs even before he asks. She realized early that the success

EVERYBODY NEEDS SOMEBODY SOMETIME

of those around her aided her own success. It is in this spirit that she serves her boss. Her dedication and excellent service to him has resulted in an interesting phenomenon.

Frequently when he has a difficult decision to make, he asks her to come into his office. Promptly she responds—not with a pencil and pad or a cup of coffee, but with some requested advice. She has his total respect and is treated accordingly in the office. (Besides, usually he follows her advice!) This secretary has been officially appointed as advisor to the president. Even though this was not part of her original job description, she acquired her authority by *serving* him.

My third example is a minister and a most unusual man. Awkward in leading services, he definitely lacks eloquence in the pulpit; and his personal appearance is not always what it should be. Yet, his services are packed, and the church is growing rapidly. The people in his congregation follow his teachings implicitly and hold him in highest regard as *their pastor.*

One night we began discussing this subject while eating supper at a local hamburger shop. I asked him why his ministry was so successful. His straightforward answer revealed a calm sense of confidence.

"As a minister, I serve the Lord first," he stated. "The things I preach or do are not always popular, but if I know they are from the Lord, I don't hesitate."

That was his answer. He reports first to his heavenly Shepherd, not to his sheep. No wonder he serves his sheep so well. He, too, is a man under authority.

As we continued our conversation, he spotted a young couple from his church sitting in another booth. He excused himself and walked over to them. I watched with

PHASE 4: MAINTENANCE

fascination as he warmly shook the fellow's hand and tenderly patted the young woman's shoulder. Then the couple appeared to be arguing about something. My friend reached into his pocket and pulled out his wallet. Opening it, he handed the couple some money. They both smiled and waved as he returned to our table.

"Well, there goes my golf game for the week, but those kids are worth it!" he said with a warm smile as he sat down.

"Why?" I inquired.

"I guess it was of the Lord that I went over to speak to them," he replied.

Continuing, he told me that they were newlyweds whom he had married several weeks before and hadn't seen since they returned from their honeymoon. After eating they had found themselves without money to pay the check, each assuming that the other one was paying. To help them avoid an argument and to have a good excuse to give them a welcome home gift, this pastor bought their supper.

With sincere satisfaction, he concluded, "This beats a golf game any day in my book."

Here we see the lesson again. This minister—because he serves the Lord—serves his people. Paying for that supper was probably his best sermon for the week. He knows the secret of service, and consequently he receives true authority as a pastor.

PAUSE TO SMELL THE FLOWERS

To maintain a relationship, think of the nurture and care a flower is given. Its health and beauty come from the attention it receives. Spend time with your relation-

EVERYBODY NEEDS SOMEBODY SOMETIME

ships. Give them your attentive care. Relationships are built on experiences together, and experiences require time. Take time to talk, to go fishing, or to work on a project together. Remember, the beauty of a relationship is directly related to the careful attention you give it.

As with a flower, your relationship also needs to be nurtured. To nurture means "to feed." Communication is the "food" that feeds your relationships. If you do not talk to your friends, your friendships will wither and die just as will plants without water. Let me remind you that communication is not only verbal. You speak with your actions, your touch, and dozens of other ways that show the other person how much you care.

Communication is also listening. Listen carefully with understanding. Besides listening to what you hear, also listen with your eyes and your intuitive feelings. With patient sensitivity receive those nonverbal messages sent through the expression and behavior of the other person. Be aware of what *you* are feeling *from* the other person as you listen. That intuitive part of you is usually an accurate reader of those nonverbal messages coming both directly and indirectly from the other individual.

A flower is not fully appreciated unless its fragrance is smelled and its beauty perceived. Beauty, indeed, is in the eyes of the beholder. Stop someday and really appreciate a flower. Look closely at its petals and observe its vivid colors painted to perfection. Smell deeply, allowing the fragrance to permeate your very being. Care and nurture are not enough. You have not fully experienced a flower until you pause to appreciate its beauty.

In similar fashion, I invite you to pause to appreciate your relationships. Take time to really get to know the other person. Learn the lessons about life that he or she

PHASE 4: MAINTENANCE

has for you. Everyone has something special to offer you if you take the time to discover it.

I learned this lesson early in my life from a man named Ole Anderson. Part of my curiosity about him stemmed from the fact that very few people in town, if any, really knew him. This eccentric old man, with a long white beard, lived a virtual hermit's life in his shabby run-down jewelry store. Actually, the store was more like a second-rate pawn shop. Hardly anyone ever entered his store, and he really didn't seem to care. I don't know how he stayed in business. He could usually be observed sitting near the front window hunched over a workbench, repairing a pocket watch that some farmer would occasionally bring to him.

Sometimes my friends and I would get too noisy while playing in front of his shop. In anger Ole would come out yelling and waving his cane. Frightened to death, we would scatter in all directions. It would take several days before we had the courage to go near his place again.

Then one day my curiosity took complete control. Standing alone in front of Ole's shop, I mustered up all the courage I had, took a deep breath, and walked straight through his front door. My first thought was that it was terribly quiet inside. Only the ticking of a stately grandfather clock broke the silence. The air smelled musty. I walked over to a dusty showcase filled with a fascinating assortment of knives, old coins, some rings and watches, and a shiny silver horse. I stood there gazing.

My attention was drawn away from these unusual objects by Ole's eyes peering down at me from the other side of the showcase.

"What do you want, boy?" he gruffly inquired.

EVERYBODY NEEDS SOMEBODY SOMETIME

"How much is that silver horse?" I nervously asked.

"It's not for sale," he replied.

"Oh, I probably couldn't afford it anyway," I responded even more timidly.

"But, I'll trade you something for it," he said.

As I stared directly into his steel-blue eyes through those thick, wire-rimmed glasses, I was about to make my first business deal.

"What do you want?" I asked with a little more confidence.

"What do you have?" he retorted.

Glancing back into that dusty showcase, I remembered that I had an old jackknife and a couple of coins from Norway at home. I told Ole that I would be right back. I sprinted the five blocks home and back again in record time. After some hearty bargaining, he had my knife and two Norwegian coins. In exchange I had the silver horse and a pocket watch that really worked. At first I thought I had gotten the best deal, but a couple of days later I began to wonder when the watch quit running and the silver began to peel off the plastic horse.

Returning to complain, I remember Ole's saying, "A deal is a deal. You made it. You stick with it."

Reflecting on that childhood experience, I now realize that I did get the best part of the deal. In those moments, years before my time, I grew up in a small but important way. Ole taught me the lesson of being responsible for my own decisions. Some would be good; others would be bad.

I also got to know personally an eccentric old Norwegian jeweler who really wasn't eccentric at all. He was kind, friendly (in his own way), and he appreciated a good business deal. We became good friends, and frequently

PHASE 4: MAINTENANCE

over the next few years I would stop by his shop to see him.

Take time to really get to know the people in your life. Pause to appreciate your friends. They each will teach you something special.

8

Phase 5: Ending

His mother was dying. Since entering the hospital a week before, she had gone steadily downhill.

"Yesterday morning the doctor told us there was nothing more they could do except try to make Mom comfortable. Hour after hour Dad sat by her bed, holding her hand, his eyes fixed on her expressionless face. She had been conscious for only a moment a couple of hours earlier. Then she lapsed back into her coma. I could only stay by her bed for a short while. Then I'd have to leave. I couldn't decide which hurt me more, to see Mom lying there near death or to see Dad's grief-filled face as they spent their last moments of life together.

"Although Mom had been ill off and on for years, she was really quite healthy until last week when she had her attack. She was rushed to the hospital where she received excellent care. For a short time the doctors were giving us favorable reports. But then their story began to change. We didn't want to believe them, but today there was no doubt in our minds that they were correct. Mom was going in and out of consciousness. Her breathing had become very labored.

PHASE 5: ENDING

"Evening was nearing as the cast of twilight came over the city. Realizing that neither Dad nor I had eaten since early morning, I suggested we get some supper. Dad said he wasn't hungry and hung onto Mom's hand all the tighter. Then the nurse came in to take Mom's pulse. She felt around on her body and listened to her chest with the stethoscope. Turning to my father, she said that Mom had stabilized. She, too, suggested that this would be a good time for us to slip away to get something to eat.

"I informed the nurse that we would be at home. They should call us immediately if there were any changes in Mom's condition. Otherwise, we would be back within a couple of hours. Very reluctantly, Dad pulled himself away and slowly walked in silence down the corridor to the elevator.

"Reaching the main floor, we continued in silence as we made our way through the lobby, crowded with individuals caught up in the dramas of their own lives. It was dark as we stepped out onto the street. Our faces were greeted by a cold drizzling rain.

"After finding the car near the back of the lot, I told Dad that I would drive. He didn't reply but silently walked around to the passenger's side and got in. As the engine idled for a moment, I turned on the radio. Dad spoke his first words since we left.

" 'Turn it off!'

"The silence continued as we made our way home. Our minds and hearts were still with Mom at the hospital. I was totally preoccupied, but somehow the car found its way and we pulled into the driveway. Everything was unusually dark and quiet. Mom was the one

EVERYBODY NEEDS SOMEBODY SOMETIME

who always had the light on for anyone who might be coming.

"Like a robot Dad shuffled in the back door, hung his coat on the familiar old worn hook, and plunked himself down at the kitchen table. This has been his routine for over forty-eight years of married life, so why should tonight be any different? I asked him what he'd like to eat. He didn't reply.

"Instinctively, I walked over to the refrigerator and opened the door to see what I could find. Inside was a dish with a cover on it, apparently leftovers from an earlier meal. Next to the dish were two whole wheat rolls wrapped in aluminum foil. Lifting the cover of the dish, I found two pieces of swiss steak, gravy, and a couple of potatoes. While it was warming on the stove, I set out two plates and some silverware. Dad just sat there in his usual place, waiting to be served.

"As the meal warmed, the aroma from the steak and gravy filled the kitchen. This had always been Mom and Dad's favorite dish. After filling our plates, we sat down to eat. With bowed heads Dad, as usual, led in prayer, thanking God for the food. Then, with tears streaming down his face, he looked directly at me and said, 'Thank you, Mama, for the swiss steak and whole wheat rolls.'

"Even while Mom was lying in the hospital dying, she saw to it that we were fed and that Dad got his favorite dish. As we ate, we savored the food for we both knew that this was the last time in our lives we would taste this meal. Only Mom knew exactly the way to prepare the meat, the gravy, and the rolls.

PHASE 5: ENDING

"Tonight Mom was dying. Farewell to swiss steak and whole wheat rolls."

Later that night, this man's mother did die. Relationships continually end. Mothers die. Friends move away. George resigns to take another job. Or sometimes, for some unexplainable reasons, you just stop seeing a good friend. Ending is part of the predictable pattern of relationships. Some relationships are for a lifetime, and others are for eternity. (I will talk about these near the end of this chapter.) But in the human, day-to-day course of events, most relationships eventually end.

THE EMOTIONS OF ENDING RELATIONSHIPS

When relationships end, you feel it. During the attraction phase you sense something within you being born. In the ending phase you perceive something within you dying. Though the dying of an unpleasant relationship may bring relief, in most relationships the ending phase inspires sadness and melancholia. Barbra Streisand captured this emotion in the hit tune and film *The Way We Were.* What you really experience when a relationship ends is not just the ceasing of the relationship itself, but the dying of a part of yourself.

Recall that relationships are built on shared experiences. Those experiences cannot be duplicated merely by substituting another person or recreating similar events. When that special person leaves, the experiences you shared are over. The ending of a relationship closes a

EVERYBODY NEEDS SOMEBODY SOMETIME

chapter in your life. What you did and felt during that relationship will be put away in the files of your memory, to be recalled occasionally when you reminisce.

I will always remember the final football game of my senior year in high school. What remains strong in my memory is not the game itself, but rather the taking off of my shoulder pads for the last time. At that moment I realized, since I was not going to play in college, that I would never suit up for a football game again. As I ended my relationship with the members of the football team, I ceased to be a football player. This is now filed as part of my past.

Another poignant ending in my life was finalized as I emptied my room at Tanis House the day following college graduation. As I said farewell to each of the guys whom I had been so close to for over two years, we realized that we would leave behind certain feelings, behavior, and experiences that undoubtedly were appropriate for only that setting.

Let your memory do some wandering. You will find some situations similar to those above and the feelings to go along with them.

The emotions you experience in the ending of relationships can run from one extreme to the other. Some endings bring pain and sadness; others bring relief and joy. Remember telling yourself that you only had to work with a certain person for another two weeks? Or the times when nobody's words seem to have the same effect as those of the friend you just lost? Your emotional reaction to the ending of a relationship is an excellent indicator of what you have experienced within that relationship.

PHASE 5: ENDING

Unattractive relationships are often controlling ones, limiting self-expression. The freedom felt in such endings contrasts with the sadness accompanying the ending of good relationships. When good times end you feel deprived; something has been taken from you, and your freedom to enjoy a pleasure has been limited. After my last high school football game, I was prevented from being a player on an organized team. The experience of feeling limited is not always applicable, but recognizing it is often a helpful way to understand your feelings.

In ending relationships your turbulent emotions or sense of loss are part of a natural, predictable pattern. *An unnecessary problem occurs when the ending of a relationship goes unacknowledged by one or both of the persons involved in it.* The individuals just drift apart without any discussion of what is happening between them. When this happens, you leave yourself wide open to misunderstandings, confusion, distrust, and a sense of rejection.

The manner in which you end a relationship is as important to the memory of that relationship as everything that occurred within its lifetime. Do not let the beautiful experiences degenerate into distrust and confusion because you neglected to properly end the relationship. Endings are not easy. How often have we either personally said or heard someone else say, "I hate goodbyes." Really, though, endings are the final tribute you can give to what the two of you shared. Neglecting this phase tends to depreciate all that you had together. Let's look at how you can effectively end your personal relationships.

EVERYBODY NEEDS SOMEBODY SOMETIME

PRINCIPLES FOR ENDING RELATIONSHIPS

The list is not long. There are really only two major guidelines, neither of which should ever be neglected.

1. Recognize together, with the other person or group of persons, that your relationship is coming to an end.

The positive effects created by proper recognition of the ending of a relationship are vividly portrayed in my couples' therapy groups. In this controlled situation, the relationships remain very real. Again and again I experience with the group the healthy process of a couple's announcing their leaving.

"We will no longer be coming to the group. This will be our last night."

After an exchange of feelings and evaluations between the departing couple and the group, the couple is sent off with warm wishes. Everyone has had an opportunity to express his thoughts before the couple leaves the group. There is seldom confusion or distrust. Although some may not agree with the couple's decision to leave, a sense of mutual respect for *their* choice to end the group relationship pervades.

It may appear easy to be straightforward in the controlled atmosphere of group therapy, but similar methods are effective in ending your personal relationships. The first thing to do when you know the relationship is coming to an end is to *talk openly about it and clearly state your reasons.*

Jesus sets the example for us in the fourteenth chapter

PHASE 5: ENDING

of the Gospel of John. With wisdom and sensitivity, Jesus told the twelve disciples, his closest companions for three years, that a part of their relationship together was coming to an end. He talked about leaving before it happened so that when the ending occurred the disciples would accept it. "And now I have told you before it comes to pass, that when it comes to pass, you may believe."[1]

2. End your relationships with gratitude,
   recognizing the benefits you realized together.

Relationships are generally formed for the mutual benefit of the persons involved. Therefore, recognize benefits accrued when the time comes for the relationship to end. Along with this recognition, express gratitude for what you have received and been permitted to give. I assure you, this is not easy; but it is extremely worthwhile. *Tell* the other person what the relationship meant to you. The value in verbalizing rests not with your eloquence, but rather with your sincerity. Your own words will say it best.

Funerals mark the ending of a life and the relationships that existed between the deceased and his family and friends. Some funerals are overcast with mourning and sadness, focusing only on the emptiness of life without that person. Other funerals become a celebration of the deceased person's life. There is rejoicing in knowing of the person's presence with the Lord. After attending both types of services, many of us would agree that the celebration of life gives a special dignity to the memory of the deceased.

Walking away from your relationships, omitting the

EVERYBODY NEEDS SOMEBODY SOMETIME

open expressions of gratitude, denies you a most special experience. Furthermore, you are leaving the relationship open for false assumptions, feelings of rejection, distrust, and disillusionment. Honestly facing the ending of a relationship may cause anguish, but walking away from it is neither an honest nor painless (in the long run) choice.

CHANGING RELATIONSHIPS—AN ENDING OF A RELATIONSHIP IN DISGUISE

There are times when a relationship with a person ends, but an association continues. The individual remains the same, yet the relationship changes. These transitions are really endings in disguise, though immediate recognition of the phase does not occur because the person is still around. Actually a new relationship with that same person has replaced the old one.

Three common examples of transitional relationships are (1) your close friend becoming a casual one, (2) your coworker being promoted, and (3) your children growing up. Let's look at each of these.

A Close Friend Becomes a Casual One

I have said that relationships are built on shared experiences and are formed and maintained by meeting one another's needs. When the experiences stop and the needs change, the relationship as you have known it ends.

If there were ever an ending that needs to be recognized openly, it is the one that happens when a strongly committed relationship evolves into one with limited commitment.

PHASE 5: ENDING

When these unplanned changes are not fully understood by both persons, a feeling of rejection is a surety.

During my high school days I had a best friend who lived just one block from my house. A day didn't go by without our being in contact with each other. Daily we rode to school together, either on my motor scooter or in his old Chevy. We played on the same football team, held down the trumpet and baritone sections of the band, and helped each other through algebra.

Then our lives changed dramatically as we graduated and went off to separate colleges. We each married following graduation and pursued careers in different parts of the country.

I often thought that if we could only live nearer one another we could continue our close friendship. My wish came true. He and his family were transferred, and they now live only a few miles from us. However, the close friendship has never revived. There are no hard feelings. In times of crisis we are still the first to be in contact with each other. Yet, over the months we seldom even get together. Why?

Our needs and experiences have changed, taking us into new and different relationships. My association with this person as a close daily friend came to a natural end. Our new relationship is casual—a level of commitment with which we are both comfortable.

Life is filled with these changes for all of us. Take the time and make the effort to understand them. Don't let a lack of communication or a false sense of rejection cheat you out of the beautiful relationship you once enjoyed with this person or the pleasant association you can now continue to have.

EVERYBODY NEEDS SOMEBODY SOMETIME

The Other Guy Gets Promoted

Ted was definitely just one of the boys. Every morning at ten, he rounded up the gang for the midmorning coffee break. Everyone liked him. He kept us going. We would always banter with Ted about his natural leadership qualities as we moved in one accord toward the cafeteria. We also pointed out his shrewdness in habitually getting someone else to pay for his coffee and doughnut!

Eventually these talents paid off for Ted. The administration saw his good qualities and put them to better use in the company. We didn't begin to realize what this promotion would mean to us personally until the day we completely missed our coffee break.

About a week after Ted's promotion to the executive wing, he stopped by our department to say hello. He said he really missed the coffee breaks with the guys. In response we enthusiastically invited him to join us. However, to our shock it wasn't the same anymore. We couldn't complain about the administrators that morning—one of them was sitting right there among us! Our relationship with Ted as "one of us" had ended. Yet, Ted was still around.

The natural course of events caused Ted to come down to see us less frequently as he formed new relationships in the executive wing. He, too, seemed to recognize that he now had less in common with us.

Then the day came when we had a major problem in our division. We needed someone in the administration to look out for our interests. Ted came through for us in a beautiful way. He accurately presented our situation to the board and saw to it that our needs were met. All in all,

PHASE 5: ENDING

Ted was still there, but our relationship with him had changed. He was no longer one of the guys who had coffee with us; rather he was our friend in the executive wing. His loyalty and care were still functioning, but in new and different ways.

Parents and Their Growing Children

Remember when your child was small. Recall that soft, high-pitched voice and the little body that crawled onto your lap. There were times when your child would ride on your shoulders or sit on your foot, laughing with glee as you moved your leg up and down. Those are happy memories for every parent.

Oftentimes you are unaware of the passing years and the changes that accompany them until you open a drawer to an old chest and pull out an outfit that your child wore only a few years ago. Or you may see a photograph of one of your children that was left in the camera for six months before it was finally developed. The change in his or her appearance in that short time leaves you shaking your head. Then you have the opportunity to hold someone's newborn baby and are jolted into the reality that your child is seven-going-on-eight years old. Immediately, it all comes back. Those feelings—that baby aroma—everything is right there. And so is the realization that your children are growing up.

I have often wondered why, in the natural course of a child's growing to maturity, there is such a struggle in many families. As a counselor and as one who served as a juvenile probation officer for three years, I am well aware of the familiar explanations: the adolescent's battle for

EVERYBODY NEEDS SOMEBODY SOMETIME

independence, the parents strictness, and peer pressure. But there is something more.

The inevitable happened when Judy and I personally joined the ranks of the parents of adolescent children. Suddenly, our eyes were opened. We felt sad. Peter, our little boy, was gone. All the activity and fun we had enjoyed with him as a little child vanished. We didn't hear his high voice, see his toys, or tuck him into bed as we had done for so many years. There was almost a sense of mourning over our little boy who was gone forever.

Yet, on the other hand, a new Peter had replaced the old one around our house. He looked and acted somewhat like the Peter we had known, but he was definitely different. His voice was lower, he sat in *my* chair to read the evening paper, and as he walked through the house you could hear his heavy footsteps. Peter the adult had replaced Peter the child.

As an adult, his perception of us as parents changed. He recognized more clearly our strengths and weaknesses. As time goes on, Peter is becoming an exciting companion whom Judy and I wouldn't trade for anything. We miss Peter the child; but for the lifetime ahead we prefer Peter the adult.

Anyone who has growing children knows the feelings I have just described. Your relationship with a child ends. Unconsciously you pass through a period of grief during the child's early adolescence, when you realize your child is gone for good. You may find yourself really missing that little one who would listen and obey. Another challenge is created in getting to know this "new person" in your family who tries to think for himself. However, look-

PHASE 5: ENDING

ing openly at what is happening, you would not want it any other way. As your child grows and matures, a new relationship is formed that provides you with a lifetime adult companion.

From these three examples of relationships that change, a common conclusion can be reached. The activities and ways you relate to others can take on new forms. In many instances you may no longer relate to each other at all. You just are not in close touch. Yet when handled properly, care and respect can be retained throughout many changes.

My childhood friend is still there if I need him, even though we are not close. Ted is still loyal to the men in his old division; however, now the loyalty is expressed in new ways from the executive wing rather than during those midmorning coffee breaks. The close love and devotion between parents and children can remain and grow even stronger after the children leave home.

RELATIONSHIPS THAT SHOULD END

Thus far I have dealt with relationships that come to an end naturally and the way they should be handled. There are also relationships that, in the best interests of the persons involved, should end. What kind of relationships are these? That decision is up to you, but here are some guidelines to help with the decision.

1. Your experiences within this relationship are generally painful and unpleasant.

EVERYBODY NEEDS SOMEBODY SOMETIME

When your relationships have an overloaded unpleasant side and weak benefits, an ending should be considered. Examples can be found in a one-sided friendship, a job in which you are miserable most of the time you are there, or any other relationship where rewards are just not present.

2. This relationship brings out the worst in you.

Each personal relationship stimulates us in different ways. Our associations with people involve various aspects of our personality and behavior, sometimes against our will. If this specific relationship consistently brings out the worst in you, it may be a relationship you need to end. As you weigh the negative side, be sure to consider your attitudes, feelings, and—definitely—your behavior.

3. This relationship creates a major conflict in other relationships you highly value.

When one relationship creates serious conflict within your other valued relationships, serious consideration must be given to ending it. Often in my practice I have seen strong healthy relationships sacrificed as a person hangs on to a destructive one. The assumption is false that the strength of your healthy relationships will remain as this other relationship destructively works its way further into your life.

SOME RELATIONSHIPS ARE NOT MEANT TO END

In this chapter on ending relationships it is a joy to declare to you that some relationships are not meant to

PHASE 5: ENDING

end. As I mentioned at the beginning of the chapter, some relationships are for a lifetime. Others are for eternity. Yes, there are some good friendships in which you remain actively involved with each other from childhood, throughout your entire life. These relationships are rare. If you have one, take good care of it. It is priceless!

We all need at least one constant human relationship with which to grow throughout our lifetime. This is where marriage comes into the picture. God brings two people together in a special way. With a total, unconditional, permanent commitment, He unites them for a lifetime. Divorce destroys this permanence. Take good care of your marriage. It can be your lifetime friendship. Although it is priceless from the beginning, its value continues to increase year by year.

Then there is the church—the believers united together in one body through their shared faith in the Lord Jesus Christ. Their relationship with one another and their heavenly Father begins in this lifetime and continues on for eternity. If you are a believer, and thus part of the church already, continue daily to care for this very special relationship you have, and thank God for it. If you do not have this eternal relationship, invite Jesus Christ into your life as your Lord and Savior. By your prayer of commitment, God through His Spirit will enter and transform your life, giving you that eternal relationship with Him and other believers that make up the body which is the church.

Here is His promise: "For God so loved the world that He gave His only begotten Son, that whoever believes in Him should not perish but have everlasting life."[2]

Once you have committed your life to God's Son, you

EVERYBODY NEEDS SOMEBODY SOMETIME

are a believer; and the relationship with the triune God *is* eternal. Nothing will separate you from His love.

> For I am convinced that nothing can ever separate us from his love. Death can't, and life can't. The angels won't, and all the powers of hell itself cannot keep God's love away. Our fears for today, our worries about tomorrow, or where we are—high above the sky, or in the deepest ocean—nothing will ever be able to separate us from the love of God demonstrated by our Lord Jesus Christ when he died for us.[3]

9

Restoring Relationships

A surge of apprehension rushed through Ann's body as she spotted Carmen seated at their usual table in a local restaurant. What an unusual reaction to seeing an old friend.

Or was it?

It had initially been Ann's idea to meet Carmen for breakfast. Furthermore, it had been a Friday morning ritual for the two of them for over six months. Yet the last of those regular breakfast meetings had occurred over one year ago. Today's meeting was different.

Ann and Carmen's story opens almost two years earlier when these two women met for the first time. Ann, as chairman of a search committee, had been working diligently to find a new director for the organization. Although her committee had interviewed dozens of candidates for this important position, it had not found anyone suitable.

This is when Carmen came on the scene. She had been highly recommended by another individual who felt the organization would be fortunate if she accepted the position. Ann met with Carmen and was favorably impressed. There was an immediate attraction between them. Ann

EVERYBODY NEEDS SOMEBODY SOMETIME

especially liked Carmen's ability to listen and to convey the feeling that what she heard was important and interesting.

Within a matter of weeks Carmen was standing before the entire membership giving her inaugural address. Everyone seemed satisfied and optimistic with her new leadership. Ann, too, was pleased, but she carried a secret concern regarding the tremendous burden of problems Carmen was inheriting along with her position.

To assist Carmen in becoming familiar with her new responsibilities as director, the search committee continued to function for an additional six months as Carmen's advisory committee. On her own, Ann suggested to Carmen that the two of them meet weekly to discuss informally any questions she had.

Carmen quickly accepted the offer, and thus the routine of sharing Friday morning breakfast began. Their regularity even caused the waitress to hold the same table by the window for them. Over cheese omelets and muffins, Carmen learned the "behind the scenes" operation of the organization in which Ann had been active for years. Each Friday Carmen would come with her list of questions. And each week Ann would provide the answers along with her opinions.

However, as time passed Carmen's list grew shorter, but the meetings grew longer. The two women talked less about official business and more about personal subjects. Ann found that she benefited from Carmen's wisdom and insight in her personal life. The two were no longer merely associates but also good friends.

Six months passed quickly, and Carmen was doing well in her position. She was demonstrating her abilities, and

RESTORING RELATIONSHIPS

age-long problems were being solved in the organization through her innovative ideas. As previously agreed, the advisory committee announced that they would disband, bringing to a conclusion a year of hard work in recruiting and orienting a new director. Ann was pleased with how well Carmen had been accepted by all the members.

The only criticism Ann had heard was that some people felt she and Carmen were becoming too close. Those voicing the criticism were implying that Ann might be overinfluencing Carmen. In an effort to protect Carmen from any unnecessary criticism so early in her term, Ann decided to discontinue their weekly meetings. She decided against discussing such petty criticism with Carmen, hoping it would die when the two of them stopped meeting regularly. Therefore, Ann suggested to Carmen that they no longer meet weekly for breakfast but instead get together whenever either one of them wanted to do so. Carmen agreed.

Weeks passed, and neither one was in personal contact with the other. Ann continued to see Carmen at the general meetings where they exchanged brief greetings as they passed in the crowd.

Eventually Ann noticed that she was consciously avoiding Carmen by leaving the auditorium through an out-of-the-way exit. Ann realized that it was less painful to say nothing at all than to exchange ritualistic greetings with someone whom she used to talk with for hours. Finally Ann allowed the press of other business to keep her away from the meetings altogether. Months passed, and the two women never saw or talked with each other.

Ann had become inactive in the organization. Often thoughts of Carmen would come to her mind, especially

EVERYBODY NEEDS SOMEBODY SOMETIME

on Friday mornings as she drove past their favorite restaurant. One day she realized that it had been over a year since she had seen or heard from Carmen. Yet, they lived in the same city, and Ann was still a member of the organization.

At times Ann continued to think of a commitment she had made to herself to support Carmen in a special way as director. She also missed those Friday morning breakfasts. What had begun as a great friendship had now come to an end, and she hadn't even consciously realized it!

All this prompted Ann to give Carmen a call. She was nervous as she dialed that once familiar number. This reaction alone assured Ann that something had gone wrong with the relationship. During those days when they were close, they had talked with each other on the telephone several times a day.

As the phone was ringing, Ann sensed ambivalence as she found herself hoping no one would answer. But soon there was a voice on the other end.

"Hello," Carmen said.

"Hi, Carmen. It's been a long time," replied Ann.

Instantly Carmen recognized the voice and seemed excited.

"Can we get together sometime?" Ann inquired.

"How about tomorrow morning for breakfast?" Carmen responded. "I have another meeting, but I'm sure I can change that."

Then it dawned on Ann that it was Thursday. The timing was perfect. She and Carmen could have one of their old Friday morning breakfasts together. They agreed to meet at the usual time and place. Both had many unanswered questions on their minds.

RESTORING RELATIONSHIPS

The routine returned the next morning as Ann's car seemed to pull automatically into the restaurant parking lot. When she walked in, the same waitress greeted her and asked where she had been all these months.

Then Ann looked toward Carmen who always seemed to arrive early enough to read the morning paper. As Ann made her way to the table, Carmen looked up and smiled. There was an unusual mixture of tension and warmth as these two old friends began talking.

"I've heard many good things about what you are doing with the organization," commented Ann.

"I couldn't have done it without the help I received from you and your committee," responded Carmen.

Over breakfast they brought each other up to date on what had been happening in their busy schedules. Carmen filled Ann in on some exciting plans for the organization and subtly tried to lure her back into more active involvement. Ann appeared tempted and was pleased that Carmen was reaching out.

After finishing breakfast, they both seemed more relaxed. They joked about some of the funny things that had occurred during those early days for Carmen. Laughing till they were in tears, they continued to relive one event after another.

Suddenly there was a long inevitable silence. Both were speechless as they searched each other's eyes. As is so common with friends, although not a word had been spoken, both knew they were thinking the same thing. They had talked about the present—they had reminisced. Now there was only one matter left to discuss. One of them had to approach it.

"What ever happened to us?" Ann finally asked.

EVERYBODY NEEDS SOMEBODY SOMETIME

"I don't know!" replied Carmen, shaking her head. "We were so close, and then there was nothing."

Ann began to explain how she had decided to discontinue the weekly breakfasts because of criticism she had heard from a few of the members. Then she remembered that she had not bothered Carmen with the details at the time.

Carmen explained to Ann that she had felt they were meeting because of friendship. Yet, as soon as the committee disbanded, the Friday morning breakfasts ceased as well. Carmen then *assumed* that Ann had been friendly as part of her responsibilities as committee chairman, and that when the committee dissolved, Ann felt she was off the hook.

They gazed at each other in bewilderment. Both were realizing for the first time that their budding friendship had been plagued by a huge dose of false assumptions and misunderstandings. Ann's intent was only to help her friend. Instead it had been misinterpreted as rejection.

In turn Carmen had not wanted to bother Ann with a relationship that she *assumed* Ann did not desire. Ann had erroneously taken this as Carmen's lack of interest in their friendship. False assumptions can occur readily with good friends because both think they know the other person so totally that they don't stop to check each other out.

There was yet another question to be asked. Carmen took the initiative. "Can we continue our friendship and get together once in a while?"

"I was hoping you would ask!" Ann happily responded.

"You've always made me handle the tough ones," Carmen jestingly remarked, knowing the relationship had been restored.

RESTORING RELATIONSHIPS

This relationship never should have ended. They simply grew apart, not realizing that neglect was causing the relationship to die. Then when recognition dawned, Ann determined to try to resurrect it. Ann and Carmen came back together; and not only did they have the old relationship back, now it was better than ever.

They decided not to return to their weekly breakfasts together, but now they usually see each other several times a month. However, when a longer-than-usual period of time passes, old tensions do not recur. Both women know where they stand with each other, and the interval is not a problem. When either of them has a question regarding the way things are going, neither is reticent to pick up the phone or arrange a get-together.

Their relationship has been restored.

DO YOU HAVE A RELATIONSHIP THAT NEEDS TO BE RESTORED?

As you contemplate your past relationships, you may also have one that needs to be restored. It may have ended prematurely, and lingering unsettled feelings remain. Perhaps there was carelessness and insensitive neglect in the relationship. The decision as to whether you should make an effort to restore a relationship is very personal. *Every person and relationship is unique.* Under God's guidance pray for His will and then make your decision.

As you consider restoring a relationship that appears to have ended prematurely, here are some guidelines to help you.

EVERYBODY NEEDS SOMEBODY SOMETIME

Commitment Test

Was a commitment broken by the ending of your relationship? Have you made a promise that is now unfulfilled? The commitment test is the most important point, for it involves not only your relationship with that person but also your personal integrity. Although we live in an age of broken promises, the keeping of one's promise is still the anchor of our character and walk with God.

Susan had been an active and committed member of her growing church for years. She was a very opinionated person and would freely pass on her views to others—often with a few "stories" she had heard mixed in. As the congregation grew and her role of influence increased, she was gossiping more and serving less.

She had always had a close and open relationship with the pastor. Thus, as complaints about her tendencies toward gossip were coming to his attention more frequently, he felt confident Susan would listen and understand, if warmly confronted.

But he was wrong.

"You're out of line," she charged, as she headed for his office door. "I'm responsible to the Lord, not to you. I don't need you or anyone else to tell me what to do."

Weeks passed into months, but Susan stayed away. "It's a matter of conscience," was her alibi when friends and members of the church would ask what was keeping her away.

One Sunday morning, while visiting another church, as she had sometimes done since she left her own, the sermon topic was "The Church That Cares." Through the message, God spoke to Susan about her problem. She

RESTORING RELATIONSHIPS

realized that part of the role of a caring church is to guide people in their walk with the Lord and when necessary confront them with their behavior.

The following week she phoned her pastor for an appointment. Received warmly by him, Susan asked for forgiveness and was restored in her commitment to the church. Once again she enjoyed the peace she had known with Christ and His people.

If you have broken a promise or commitment, consider renewing it by reaching out to the person or group you have let down. Not only will you live better with that person or group, but you will be happier with yourself.

Needs Test

You will recall that all relationships are formed and maintained when the parties involved meet one another's needs. Are there needs that are going unmet by the premature ending of the relationship in question? In certain relationships once the needs have been fulfilled, the appropriate ending often follows.

Recall from the commitment chapter that Charlie agreed to be with Lance throughout Lance's political campaign. This was when Charlie was needed. Once the campaign was over, that need no longer existed. Therefore, Charlie's commitment had been fulfilled, and the relationship as both Charlie and Lance knew it came to an end.

Conversely, if you have a need that once was met by a relationship that since has ended and this need continues unfulfilled, you may wish to consider restoring the old relationship. In the natural course of events you will

EVERYBODY NEEDS SOMEBODY SOMETIME

either seek to renew the old relationship or you will develop a new one to meet that need.

A woman who was married for over twenty-two years shocked her husband with a quick divorce. She left because she was bored, lonely, and wanted more exciting companionship. Ten months later she found herself sitting *alone* in her apartment, again bored, lonely, and looking for exciting companionship. She had dated several men, but none were as exciting and good-looking as her ex-husband!

Whenever she met a man similar to her former husband, she would date him. As a matter of fact, if any of these men had proposed, she probably would have married him. She knew by now that she enjoyed and needed married life. Then it dawned on her to go back to her ex-husband. She did; and after months of courting, as well as seeking counsel with me, they restored their marriage. She learned that, along with her broken commitment, her needs were met best within that relationship. And she learned that one of *her* needs was to meet *his* needs. They made some changes in an effort to do better in the "need meeting areas," and their efforts have paid off handsomely.

Effect-on-Others Test

What effect did the ending of your relationship have upon others in your life? In itself this definitely is not the basis for restoring a relationship, but it should be a consideration. Were others hurt to the extent that you also feel the effects?

Two professional people I know practiced together for

RESTORING RELATIONSHIPS

years. Their clients came to relate to them as a team. Then they discontinued their partnership and opened separate offices. Their clientele had a terrible time determining whom to see, and as a result of their own indecision they referred others to the two less frequently. Apparently the confidence others placed in them when they worked together didn't carry over to their private practices.

After carefully analyzing the impact the ended relationship had upon others and upon themselves, the two former partners determined to reunite. Within a few months their practice was back to normal.

Recall Test

Do you find it difficult to get a former friend and old relationship out of your thoughts? If you continually are recalling someone, your mind may be suggesting the unsettledness of that relationship.

Let me caution you again that this recall test in and of itself is insufficient for determining if a relationship should be restored. Many relationships that appropriately end remain in our minds as a pleasant memory. Similarly many unhappy or ill-conceived relationships remain in our minds as an unpleasant memory. However, if you frequently recall an unsettled aspect, you may have some unfinished business with that person.

Ending Test

How did your relationship end? A relationship that prematurely ends can often be identified by an absence of

EVERYBODY NEEDS SOMEBODY SOMETIME

an ending, or a bad ending. Oftentimes, however, two people just grow apart. Days pass into weeks and weeks into months. In Ann and Carmen's experience, an entire year went by without any contact between them.

Other times a relationship may come to a violent and abrupt end, possibly through an unresolved argument. In this case it may take the supreme effort of setting aside your pride to restore the relationship. Reaching out after a disagreement does not necessarily mean that you are giving in to the other person's point of view. It merely indicates that you believe your relationship is more important than the issue in question. Married couples who come in for counseling develop this skill during therapy. Arguments quickly diminish in importance as the couple learns to focus first on their relationship and then on the issues in question.

If an ending is violent, vague, or totally missing, you may need to consider restoring the relationship.

HOW TO RESTORE A BROKEN RELATIONSHIP

Because each relationship is unique, the process for restoring one must be individually tailored to its particular characteristics. Your discernment will be best here since you know the relationship better than anyone else. Being your natural self is paramount to your choice of finding the most suitable approach or technique to use. If you are phony, I guarantee that your efforts will go nowhere. Within the spontaneity of your approach, here are some rules that will help you to be successful.

RESTORING RELATIONSHIPS

Personally Meet With the Other Person

A direct, personal, face-to-face contact with the other person is best. As you communicate about sensitive matters, eye contact and nonverbal messages are an important part of the exchange. A confrontation also implies that you value the relationship.

Allow Sufficient Time to Say It All

When a person is interrupted in the middle of a message, it will seem like rejection. If it is impossible to get together for a long enough period of time to deal sufficiently with the entire situation, agree on a time and place to resume talking. This will assure the other person that you are interested in hearing him out.

Keep Your Meeting Free From Distractions

Oftentimes a discussion is thwarted by constant outside interruptions. This should not imply, however, that you need complete privacy. For Ann and Carmen the best setting was at the familiar restaurant with other people sitting at tables around them.

Be Prepared to Listen

Most likely you will have much to say. But remember, so does the other person. Most people want to be heard, but force yourself to listen first. This demonstrates acceptance and will begin to reopen the relationship. You also may learn some new information to help you better understand what happened.

EVERYBODY NEEDS SOMEBODY SOMETIME

Understand Before You Explain

Understanding the other person's situation and point of view is a great healing salve for a relationship. Realize that understanding the other person's viewpoint does not mean you are agreeing with or approving it. You simply are saying that you can perceive how he or she came to that position. If you cannot understand, at least make the effort and then tell the other person you would *like* to understand. This is not as helpful as true understanding, obviously, but it runs a close second.

Present Your Feelings and Needs First

After you have listened with understanding, give your side of what happened. First, present how you feel and what you need from the relationship. Then talk about the facts and opinions. Feelings and needs cannot really be disputed. For example, Carmen *felt* that Ann did not wish to continue their relationship. No one could dispute Carmen's feelings, although they were not factually correct. Basing her case on a rational judgment that Ann did not want to continue the relationship would have been fertile ground for a difference of opinion. Only Carmen knew her own feelings about the situation, but Ann knew her own intentions of maintaining a relationship with Carmen.

Be Able to Admit Your Mistakes

When you realize that you have made a mistake, admit it. Your pride may tell you that, by this admission, you lose. However as soon as you make the acknowledgment,

RESTORING RELATIONSHIPS

you will discover that the opposite is true. First, the difference of opinion no longer exists. Second, it demonstrates that you have the insight and character to recognize your weaknesses. In a sense, admitting a mistake or failure reflects a self-acceptance that makes you open and honest with others.

Remember that *a relationship will only be restored when the value of the relationship rises above the issues that caused the two people to part.* This concept is summarized in the brief statement, "We have too much going for us to let this come between us."

This list certainly is not all-inclusive, but it will help you to make a successful effort to restore a broken relationship. Keep in mind that you cannot restore a relationship alone. As in the initial development of a relationship, it requires the response of the other person. However, if you make the restoration effort and the other person chooses not to reestablish the relationship, your effort is not in vain. By going through this process you have properly ended the relationship as discussed in the previous chapter. Then you should be able to put it to rest in your thoughts, for you have done all you can.

A VIEW FROM THE OTHER SIDE

We cannot leave this subject without looking for a moment at the process of restoration from the other side. If you are approached by someone who wishes to restore a relationship, receive that person with warmth and love. Initially you may have been hurt by this growing apart.

EVERYBODY NEEDS SOMEBODY SOMETIME

You naturally may be skeptical as a means of protecting yourself from further hurts. Endeavor to be open and to see the relationship in the present.

If the person is coming to you with feelings such as we have just discussed, you must realize that there is a basic caring for you individually and for the relationship you once shared. Give the person an honest chance. There will be benefits for both of you.

In the Gospel of Luke, chapter 15, we learn an important lesson on restoring broken relationships. In the familiar story of the prodigal son, a young man asks for his inheritance so that he can leave home to pursue his own pleasures.

Going to a far country, he squanders all his wealth on loose living. Finding himself a pauper in a time of famine, he works in the fields feeding pigs. Eventually he longs to eat even the garbage he feeds to the swine.

One day he makes a very important retrospection. He remembers that his father treats his slaves better than this. He therefore concludes that he would be better off as a servant of his father than a servant in this distant land. The son returns to his father and tells him that he is no longer worthy to be a son. He requests instead to be accepted in the household as a servant. The son wants to restore the relationship but is willing to occupy a lesser position because of his sin.

How does the father respond? What is our lesson when someone approaches us to restore a relationship?

> ... his father saw him and had compassion, and ran and embraced him and kissed him.
> ... the father said to his servants, 'Bring quickly the best

RESTORING RELATIONSHIPS

robe, and put it on him; and put a ring on his hand, and shoes on his feet; and bring the fatted calf and kill it, and let us eat and make merry; for this my son was dead, and is alive again; he was lost, and is found.'[1]

We may learn many lessons from this parable in the Bible. First of all, the son was required to set aside his pride and admit his sin when he returned to his father. Then, from the other side, we see that the son was received with love and compassion. We are not to hold grudges over past actions, but in the spirit of forgiveness we can restore the person to his proper place in the relationship. The joy, then, is on both sides. Not only was the son happy over his acceptance by his father, but the father was overjoyed to have his son back. *Coming back together brings happiness to both persons.*

We cannot go on without looking at the deeper meaning of the parable. We are the prodigal son, and God is the Father. Through our sin, we left Him and our inheritance as sons of God. Yet, the story does not end here. If we return to Him, confessing our sins, He will forgive them and restore us to a place as joint heirs of His heavenly kingdom.

Coming to a personal relationship with God through a trust and commitment to Jesus, His Son, is not a new relationship but a restored one. You are *coming back together* with your Creator, the One who loved you first and gave His Son to die on the cross for your sins.

10

Don't Go It Alone

Today they began gathering earlier than usual. From every direction cars filled with moms, dads, and kids rumbled over those familiar roads one last time to the little country church in the grove. Pulling into the churchyard, each car automatically rolled across the grass, coming to a stop randomly under the large oak trees that shaded the entire area. In the spring, tire tracks marred the churchyard, but no one seemed to mind.

Sometime around the turn of the century this church building had been erected as a place of worship by the first settlers in the area. Over the years all the important events in the lives of the local people were recognized here. Births were announced. Young lovers were wed. Funerals were held. The churchyard became the traditional site for the annual Sunday school picnic. But most important of all, people found the Lord in this little old church and grew spiritually under its care.

This church building also came to symbolize the oneness felt by the members with each other. They often argued among themselves. Sometimes their discussions really got heated. But if anyone had a problem or a need,

DON'T GO IT ALONE

the others were always ready to help. For years the church had served as the central meeting place to discuss important business matters in the area. Old-timers still tell stories about major decisions that were made "right here in this church building."

After generations, the life of this little church building was coming to an end. Tradition of the past was forced to yield to the plans of the future. This day the people that comprise the fellowship gathered in their little church for a final service.

Next Sunday everyone would need to reorient themselves. They had just plain outgrown their little church. Instead of driving the usual route to the church in the country, they would go into town to their fresh, new sanctuary awaiting its body of believers. The speaker for this special, final service was the pastor who for years had served this church so faithfully. He mentioned that he thought he had preached his last sermon in this sanctuary ten years ago when he retired from active ministry. But today he had returned one more time to preach the final sermon for this little church.

The old, white-haired pastor walked solemnly to the pulpit. Although the years had left their mark, he stood erect and his voice thundered with the authority of one accustomed to preaching God's Word. He invited the congregation to open their Bibles, and he read to them from Paul's letter to Ephesians:

> We are all parts of one body, we have the same Spirit, and we have all been called to the same glorious future. For us there is only one Lord, one faith, one baptism, and we all have the same God and Father who is over us all and in us all, and living through every part of us. However, Christ has given

EVERYBODY NEEDS SOMEBODY SOMETIME

each of us special abilities—whatever he wants us to have out of his rich storehouse of gifts....

Some of us have been given special ability as apostles; to others he has given the gift of being able to preach well; some have special ability in winning people to Christ, helping them to trust him as their Savior; still others have a gift for caring for God's people as a shepherd does his sheep, leading and teaching them in the ways of God.

Why is it that he gives us these special abilities to do certain things best? It is that God's people will be equipped to do better work for him, building up the church, the body of Christ, to a position of strength and maturity; until finally we all believe alike about our salvation and about our Savior, God's Son, and all become full-grown in the Lord—yes, to the point of being filled full with Christ.

... Under his direction the whole body is fitted together perfectly, and each part in its own special way helps the other parts, so that the whole body is healthy and growing and full of love.[1]

Peering out at the congregation over the top of his wire-rimmed glasses, he said that this portion of Scripture can be condensed into a single message from the Lord. Banging his fist against the pulpit he said with a voice that seemed to shake the old church walls, "Don't go it alone!"

I now appeal to you with this same message. Strength is not found in ourselves alone. Rather it comes from our relationships. This principle can be seen in the design of the human body, where each part is knit together to enable the body to work effectively. For instance, one's hand or arm alone is incapable of service and its value minimal. But when it is connected to the other parts of the body, it becomes functional and its value is priceless.

DON'T GO IT ALONE

This illustration is especially reflective of the body of people that make up the church. Each individual is a part of the body by virtue of his or her relationship with the Head (Christ) and with the other parts. In themselves Christians are not strong, but they grow stronger as they become a part of the whole body of Christ through the church.

Nearly a century ago the forefathers who built that little country church based their convictions and strength upon this very teaching. They knew they needed the Lord, and in turn they needed each other. Generation upon generation have now passed through this church with the same need, creating a perpetual unity that lives on among them to this very day.

This message applies to you as well. You cannot find the happiness and joy for which you are searching by going it alone. From the beginning God has told us that "'It is not good that the man should be alone....'"[2] This statement is traditionally applied to the marriage union, but I believe there is a broader meaning as well. It is not good that *mankind* should be alone. Through marriage, families, the church, and a multitude of other settings, God has designed us to live together in relationships.

Know your relationships. Understand all their phases and the uniqueness of each. Take this understanding and care for your relationships as your most valued possessions. Indeed, your relationships are priceless. *A true relationship can only be purchased by giving of yourself to the other person.* In turn you will receive the same gift. Through this beautiful process, we are to live out our lives. This is God's plan.

EVERYBODY NEEDS SOMEBODY SOMETIME

MEANWHILE, BACK AT THE RETREAT

By now the people at the retreat center were also learning in a deeper way the importance of their relationships. Many were discovering that they, too, cannot go it alone. An awareness of a vibrant love was present in these people's lives. We had become a miniature church for one week. Now the last day had arrived.

At our noon lunch, Steve, the retreat director, stood to make some announcements. He began with an unhappy one.

"I am sorry to report that we have had a theft here at the center. Harold informed me just a short while ago that sixty dollars was missing from his wallet. I don't know if anything can be done about it, but I felt you ought to know."

Harold and his family had been staying in their tent at one of the camp sites. Their budget was tight for this vacation, so the tent provided a means of reducing the cost. It had never occurred to him that his money would not be safe there. The thief had left twenty-five dollars in the wallet, apparently hoping that the stolen amount would go undetected for a while.

Steve continued the announcements. He reminded everyone that the week would officially conclude with a communion service at 9:00 P.M. Enthusiastically he told us that the service would be held at a newly constructed chapel. The building was designed especially for worship experiences of this type. We were to be the first group to use it.

A mixture of feelings seemed to be running through folks as this service was announced. Everyone felt it

DON'T GO IT ALONE

would be the highlight of the week, but they also knew it marked the end of our time together. A spirit of love and concern was evident among us after this week of being able to give ourselves totally to our relationships with the Lord, our families, and each other.

Following the announcements as we were leaving the lodge, one of the fellows approached me. He said that he was taking up a collection for Harold to help replenish the stolen sixty dollars. Readily, I reached into my pocket and found two dollars. I tossed it into the hat thinking that it really wasn't much, but it was all that I had with me at that moment. What we hadn't realized was that several others had independently initiated similar collection efforts to help Harold and his family.

For some reason I chose to take a different path back to our cabin. Walking alone, I strolled down an isolated path that led to one of the quiet, more undisturbed parts of the lake's shoreline. Eventually the path leads back around to the cabins. While absorbing the beauty of nature around me, I became aware of footsteps behind me. Turning I saw Lisa about twenty feet away. She hesitated but then spoke.

"I hope I'm not bothering you," she timidly said.

"Not at all, Lisa," I replied. "Come, walk with me."

Joining me, she confessed, "I have wanted to talk with you all week, but I couldn't decide how to put into words what I need to say. It's the last day, and I realize if I don't talk to you now, I won't have another chance."

I listened intently as she began to pour out her heart.

"I have a different kind of problem," she began.

"What is it?" I inquired.

"My husband, Paul, and I have a big block in our mar-

EVERYBODY NEEDS SOMEBODY SOMETIME

riage relationship. We deeply care about each other, but something occurred in his past that seems to block us from getting close.

"Before I knew Paul, he served in the military and was stationed in Viet Nam," she continued. "Something happened over there for which he feels terribly guilty. I don't know if he killed some people, fathered a child, or what."

"Lisa, do you need to know?" I asked.

"No! Definitely not," she emphatically replied.

"I just need to be able to let him know that he is truly forgiven. You see, Paul needs my forgiveness, but he can't even talk about what I'm supposed to forgive." As she continued her plight, nearly in tears, she said, "I don't want to force him to discuss his secret, but I really feel that he won't accept my forgiveness any other way."

"Do you understand my problem?" she asked.

"Yes, I do," I replied.

"How can I let him know that he is forgiven without forcing him to talk about this painful experience from his past?" Lisa pleaded.

Ironically, as I looked into her tear-filled eyes all I could see was forgiveness. How frustrating it is when you cannot communicate a deep feeling to someone you love. This was the tremendous hurt that Lisa was carrying.

My mind frantically searched through every logical response that I might give. Yet, I could not come up with anything really appropriate. Admitting defeat, I had to resort to those three words she didn't want to hear.

"I don't know," I reluctantly responded. The ray of hope vanished from her searching eyes.

DON'T GO IT ALONE

"But maybe God will provide a way," I added, hoping to offer some consolation.

"I don't think so," she sadly replied as she turned to walk in the other direction. "It has already been too long."

11

Go In Peace

Darkness was falling as our final day came to a close. What remained of the full moon earlier in the week was now hidden with the stars behind a heavy cloud cover. A cool misty rain added to the chill that seemed to announce the onset of fall. If you stood at just the right angle in front of a light, you could even see your breath. Summer was ending, and so was our week together.

Outside the lodge we heard the voices and saw the shadows of our group huddled together awaiting the walk over to the new chapel. As Judy and I approached the group, their warmth seemed to banish any chill we were feeling from the changing weather. Anticipation, mixed with sadness, seemed to be the mood that permeated everyone as time drew nearer for us to share our last experience together. Any tensions or guardedness that were felt earlier in the week had totally disappeared. I am always amazed at how quickly relationships become strong when you have uninterrupted time together.

Finally someone said, "What are we waiting for?"

"I don't know," replied another.

Earlier, I had decided that any leadership role I had

GO IN PEACE

possessed during the week would be over with the completion of my lecture on ending relationships earlier in the day. Tonight, I just wanted to be part of the group.

"Let's go. I'll lead the way," responded Dan.

Regardless of all the effort he had made to tone down his aggressiveness through the week, he is just a natural "take-charge" kind of person. Frankly, I guess every group needs *one*. Tonight we had Dan. Sherry, his wife, warmly hung onto his arm, evincing the closeness they had reclaimed in their marriage.

Everyone moved out following Dan and the faint beam from his flickering flashlight. He kept apologizing for the fact that someone must have carelessly left it on, nearly wearing out its batteries. Sherry was about to blurt out that he had done it himself, but this time she controlled herself by whispering it with a smile to several friends nearby.

It became totally dark as we left the lights of the lodge behind us and groped our way down the road through the woods. Every now and then, someone would yell as they either stepped into a puddle or were teasingly grabbed by an adult who for the moment turned child.

Rounding the bend we were greeted by a light from the chapel a short distance away. The glow from a stained glass window seemed to serve as a lighthouse, guiding us the remainder of the way. They had preserved this treasure from an old church that was destined for demolition.

As we walked up the stairs, the huge double doors swung open and we were greeted with a warm smile from David, a pastor who had come tonight to lead us in this

EVERYBODY NEEDS SOMEBODY SOMETIME

special communion service. Before entering, we all felt compelled to leave our wet muddy shoes outside on the stairs. Everything was so fresh and new as we entered this beautiful place of worship in the woods.

Candles were already burning around the room, and a table was prepared with the loaf of bread and the cup. The sacred holiness filling this place left no doubt that the Spirit of the Lord was present. A quiet reverence automatically overtook all of us as we found a seat and in prayer and meditation began our communion with God.

A bearded young man with a guitar softly started to sing, "There's A Sweet, Sweet Spirit in This Place." Spontaneously, we all joined in chorus. Glancing about the room, my eyes went from one person to another as they were engrossed in worship. I began to relive some of the events of the week. It was then I realized that the Lord had given me personal experiences with each individual at one time or another during the week. Not one person had been missed.

I fished with some and rode horseback with others, sailed, canoed, and even joined one fellow, on a dare, to go snorkeling in the swimming area while everyone else stood shivering on shore in jeans and sweaters. Yes, the Lord let it happen—many shared experiences during our week together.

Following the singing, Pastor David stood and asked Harold to come to the front. Neither Harold nor the rest of us knew exactly what was coming. Harold was shy, and it definitely showed as he walked up to join the pastor.

David reached out and putting his hand on Harold's shoulder said, "Today, after Steve announced that sixty dollars was stolen from your tent, several people inde-

GO IN PEACE

pendently took up a collection for you. We personally felt your loss and wanted to share it with you."

Reaching into his pocket, David pulled out some money and handed it to Harold.

"This is what was received. I don't even know how much it is, but it comes to you with our love," David continued.

"Thanks—thanks a lot!" was all that Harold could say. Emotions started to overtake him. Regaining his composure, he remained for another moment and began counting the money.

"Fifty-seven dollars! That's wonderful!" he said, as he returned to his seat.

What a vivid illustration of the church in action. I was driven to open my Bible to First Corinthians and read from chapter twelve. That chapter seemed to talk about what we had just experienced with Harold. Skimming through the chapter these words stood out:

> So God has put the body together in such a way that extra honor and care are given to those parts that might otherwise seem less important. This makes for happiness among the parts, so that the parts have the same care for each other that they do for themselves. *If one part suffers, all parts suffer with it, and if one part is honored, all the parts are glad.*[1]

Through this voluntary collection, everyone "suffered" a little but in doing so reduced Harold's suffering. Setback is never as bad when suffering can be spread out and shared by several in a caring manner.

Furthermore, these verses explained to me why Harold received fifty-seven dollars. At first I had wondered why God in His special way of handling things had not pro-

EVERYBODY NEEDS SOMEBODY SOMETIME

vided Harold with the full sixty dollars or even more. Then I realized that Harold, receiving only fifty-seven dollars, sustained his share of the loss, too.

A time of sharing followed. One person after another stood and told how God had worked with him or her during the week. My heart was blessed as I quietly sat in the back row and listened. Then Warren, the youth minister, stood holding a post card he had received in the mail.

"I received this card today. With it came my answer to the decision I told you earlier I had to make."

My mind flashed back to the orientation meeting on the first afternoon when Warren struggled to tell us about this major decision he was facing. Sensing his discouragement in ministering to young people, I was especially curious to hear what he was going to say.

Openly he told us that the kids' comments had him convinced that he was too quiet and passive to relate to them effectively. Yet, he deeply loved them and had a real burden for them in his heart.

"Just when I was ready to give up and resign, God sent me my answer by mail," he continued.

"I would like to read the card from my gang of kids back home."

Holding the card tightly, as one would cling to a valued possession, he read, "Hi, Warren. We took a vote and decided to send you this card. Hope it arrives before you leave. We just want you to know that your quiet, passive self is really missed. We hope you don't take our kidding too seriously! You listen to us and let us be ourselves. We really appreciate that. Don't change, and hurry back!"

Warren said nothing more. The card had said it all. He stood briefly, staring at the card, then quietly sat down.

GO IN PEACE

David took the loaf of bread from the table and held it up in front of him as he asked God's blessing upon it. Breaking the loaf, he repeated the words of Jesus, "... this is my body, which is broken for you."[2] Placing a piece of bread in his mouth, he passed the loaf to the person in the front row. In turn these same words were spoken by each person in the group as a piece of bread was broken and the loaf was passed. Those beautiful words never became repititious as they were spoken by different voices throughout the room—one body, many parts.

In like manner, David held up the cup and said, "Because of Jesus, your sins are forgiven." Sipping from the cup, he passed it. Reverently the cup made its way through the group. Each declared the words of forgiveness to the following person.

Paul, Lisa's husband, was sitting next to me. On the other side of him sat Lisa. A feeling of disappointment continued to linger in my mind as I reflected on my inability to help Lisa earlier in the day with her intense desire, yet inability, to show Paul forgiveness. Then the moment came.

Lisa received the cup from the person next to her and turned directly facing Paul. His back was to me, but I was facing Lisa catching the full impact of what was about to happen. Filled with love, compassion, and a new God-given confidence, she looked directly at Paul and declared, *"Because of Jesus your sins are forgiven."* Her warm loving eyes pierced deeply into Paul's as the power of God's forgiveness did its work in his life. God finally had granted Lisa the moment for which she had so patiently waited.

As Paul turned to me, tears streaming uncontrollably

EVERYBODY NEEDS SOMEBODY SOMETIME

down his face, I received the cup from a man who knew he was forgiven. He could now declare this same message to me with renewed faith and joy. Because of Jesus, he was forgiven.

The cup completed its way to the last person in the row and was carried back to the front. Our service was about over. We stood, sung a hymn, and were supposed to depart. But no one wanted to leave. We were savoring those final shared moments of unity.

Various ones started coming up to say good-bye and to thank us for the week. Henry, the man from the State Department, was one of them. Stepping up, he politely shook my hand and said his farewell.

"Thank you so much for this week. You have been most helpful in guiding me toward resolution of the problems I am facing."

I was puzzled. I never knew what his problems were nor how I had helped him. However, that was not important. Some people just seem to work out problems best on their own. Apparently Henry is one of them.

Jack and Beth were aggressively pushing their way through the crowd to Judy and me. They both had radiant smiles on their faces. Together we embraced as Jack said, "God bless." Those two words along with the embrace assured me that everything between them was fine. God had worked in their lives as well.

Finally the double doors swung open, and people started to leave. The time had come for them to return to their lives out in the world. One by one they left the warm sanctuary and stepped out into the cold, black night. But they were not alone. They had the Lord and all the relationships He would provide for them throughout their lives and eternity.

GO IN PEACE

Now as you also go on in life, do not try to go it alone. Don't be a popular person without any friends. Connect with others by moving through *attraction* and *testing* toward establishing a *committed* relationship. Develop those links with others so that they can count on you and you on them. Allow the Lord to be strong in your life, being both the Model and the Source of your commitment to one another. Take with you the five phases of relationships and make them a part of your daily life.

1. *Attraction*

Be aware of your attraction to others and why it is happening. Hold on to those newly discovered potentials within yourself as revealed by your attraction to that person. Allow your attraction to God to grow within you, as you sense His unconditional love for you.

2. *Testing*

Remember not to jump into any relationship. It needs to be checked out. Use effectively those signposts for testing, seeking the answers to availability, adjustment, and willingness to commit before you go on. Become familiar with the interplay of forces as you experience being tested by the other person at the same time you are testing. Take your rejections and transform them from endings into beginnings. We all have them.

Let me remind you that there is a cost with every relationship. But it is the cost that gives the relationship its value. As you walk with God, count the cost.

Dietrich Bonhoeffer in his book *The Cost of Discipleship* says it this way:

EVERYBODY NEEDS SOMEBODY SOMETIME

When Levi was called from the receipt of customs and Peter from his nets, there was no doubt that Jesus meant business. Both of them were to leave everything and follow. Again when Peter was called to walk on the rolling sea, he had to get up and risk his life. Only one thing was required in each case—to rely on Christ's word, and cling to it as offering greater security than all the securities in the world.[3]

3. *Commitment*

A relationship does not exist until you have a commitment. Be clear and direct with your commitment promise. This seals the relationship. When the commitment is weak, the relationship is vague. Again and again testing will reappear as you struggle to determine whether or not you have a relationship. When you are ready to commit—say it!

With the Lord the commitment step is totally yours. God made his commitment to you when He extended His unconditional love. But without your commitment to Him in return, there is no relationship.

4. *Maintaining*

In this phase, grasp the true power of *service* and use it in your relationships. The highest ideal of any relationship is serving one another. When you focus on reaching out to meet the needs of others, eventually the same will come back to you from them.

As you walk with the Lord you will serve Him. But even here it is not a one-way process. While you are serving Him, you will discover that He is serving you. His service comes through His gifts of salvation, wisdom,

GO IN PEACE

knowledge, courage, power, love, and all the fruits of the Spirit that are given generously to those who believe.

5. *Ending*

When our limited human relationships come to an end, actively end them. Don't allow yourself to drift apart from someone without acknowledging this final phase in your relationship. Recognize openly it is ending and thank the person for all that has been experienced through the relationship. Then the memory of the relationship will live on in the dignity it deserves.

The greatest news I have for you in your personal relationship with God is—*there is no ending.* It begins now with your commitment and continues for eternity. May God bless you and all the relationships He has for you.

Notes

CHAPTER 3

[1] William Glasser, *Reality Therapy* (New York: Harper & Row, 1965), p. 12.
[2] Ibid., pp. 23–24.
[3] John 3:16 RSV, italics added.

CHAPTER 4

[1] Luke 5:27,29 TLB.
[2] Acts 17:22,23 TLB.

CHAPTER 5

[1] See 2 Timothy 4:7,8.

CHAPTER 6

[1] William H. Leach, *The Cokesbury Marriage Manual* (Nashville: Cokesbury Press, 1933), p. 27.
[2] Ibid.
[3] Genesis 2:25 RSV.

CHAPTER 7

[1] Galatians 5:13,14, italics added TLB.
[2] Ephesians 6:5–9, italics added TLB.
[3] 1 Thessalonians 5:11 TLB.
[4] Luke 22:25–27, italics added TLB.
[5] John 13:4,5 TLB.
[6] Philippians 2:2–11, italics added TLB.

CHAPTER 8

[1] John 14:29 NKJB-NT.
[2] John 3:16 NKJB-NT.
[3] Romans 8:38,29 TLB.

CHAPTER 9

[1] Luke 15:20b, 22–24a RSV.

CHAPTER 10

[1] Ephesians 4:4–7, 11–13,16 TLB.
[2] Genesis 2:18 RSV.

CHAPTER 11

[1] 1 Corinthians 12:24b–26 TLB, italics added.
[2] 1 Corinthians 11:24 KJV.
[3] Dietrich Bonhoeffer, *The Cost of Discipleship* (New York: Macmillan, 1972), p. 82.